Home–School Work in Britain

review, reflection and development

by Members of the
National Home–School Development Group
edited by John Bastiani and
Sheila Wolfendale

David Fulton Publishers
London

David Fulton Publishers Ltd
The Chiswick Centre, 414 Chiswick High Road, London W4 5TF
www.fultonpublishers.co.uk

First published in Great Britain in 1996 by David Fulton Publishers

Note: The rights of John Bastiani and Sheila Wolfendale to be
identified as the authors of this work have been asserted by them in accordaɪ
with the Copyright, Designs and Patents Act 1988.

David Fulton Publishers is a division of Granada Learning Limited, part of
Granada plc.

2 00 6 004 424

British Library Cataloguing in Publication Data
A catalogue record for this book is available from the British Library.

ISBN 1-85346-395-7

Typeset by The Harrington Consultancy
Printed and bound in Great Britain

Contents

Notes on the contributors   v

Introduction *The Editors*   1

1   Managing the changing power bases – parents, schools, governors and LEAs *Alwyn Morgan*   7

2   Learning begins at home: implications for a learning society *Titus Alexander*   15

3   Good mothers are women too: the gender implications of parental involvement in education *Kathy Maclachlan*   28

4   'It hurts me in my heart when my child brings home a book' – reading at home for bilingual families *Diana Stoker*   39

5   Empowering pupils through home–school links *Conrad Chapman* 47

6   Home–school liaison: the mainstreaming of good ideas and effective practice *John Bastiani*   58

7   The PSP experience in Liverpool: towards a city-wide service *The Liverpool Parent School Partnership*   70

8   The contribution of parents to children's achievement in school: policy and practice in the London Borough of Newham *Sheila Wolfendale*   83

9   Home–school projects: influencing long-term change *Anne Houston*   95

10   Home works: shared maths and shared writing *Ruth Merttens and Alan Newland*   106

11   Making school more visible to parents: an evaluation of the Harbinger Video Project *Roger Hancock, with Anne O'Connor, Helen Jenner, Gavin Østmo and Geoff Sheath*   118

12   Setting up a parents' advice centre: partnership or PR? *Sarah Gale*   128

13   Parents and secondary schools: a different approach? *Emma Beresford and Angus Hardie*   139

14   Home to school is a long way: facing up to the issues of developing home–school alliances in rural areas *Tanny Stobart*   152

Index   164

Home and School – A Working Alliance

This Series, edited by *John Bastiani* and *Sheila Wolfendale*, brings together wide-ranging contributions which

* are written from both professional and parental viewpoints
* offer an assessment of what has been achieved
* explore a number of problematic issues and experiences
* illustrate developments that are beginning to take shape

It will appeal to those with a special interest in and commitment to home–school work in all its actual and potential facets

Early titles are:

Working with Parents as Partners in SEN
Eileen Gascoigne
1–85346–375–2

Home–School Work in Britain – review, reflection and development
By members of the National Home–School Development Group, edited by John Bastiani and Sheila Wolfendale
1–85346–395–7

Subsequent titles will include:

Home–School Liaison and Multicultural Education – making the case, supporting development, showing that it works
Edited by John Bastiani
1–85346–428–7

Working with Parents of SEN Children after the Code of Practice
Edited by Sheila Wolfendale
1–85346–429–5

Parental Perspectives and Experience
Author to be announced

Parents and Children's Learning
Author to be announced

Notes on the contributors

Titus Alexander is an independent educator, trainer and story teller. As Adviser for Community Education in London he set up a parent education programme, developed guidelines for whole-school policies for parental involvement and started an interagency strategy for supporting parents.

John Bastiani has been the coordinator of the National Home–School Development Group since its formation. A former tutor at the University of Nottingham's School of Education, he has recently been the director of the RSA's 'Parents in a Learning Society' Project. He is a member of several national advisory groups, runs INSET courses around the UK and is a freelance consultant on home–school matters.

Emma Beresford and Angus Hardie Emma worked for eight years coordinating work with parents at an inner-city secondary school. She has also undertaken research and training in this area across the country and is currently working as an adviser on partnership with parents for Manchester LEA.

Angus has worked for many years in a variety of urban regeneration programmes which have an economic and community development focus. He currently directs an Urban Programme funded project based in a Scottish secondary school which is developing innovative approaches in the field of home–school activity.

Lyn Carey, Teresa Cassidy, Fiona Chambers, Pat McCormack and Pauline Sanderson are current members of the Liverpool Parent School Partnership (PSP) service with varying perspectives on the development of the work – as outreach worker, teacher key workers, service manager and administrator. All are members of the PSP Development Team involved in leading forward the dissemination of the service.

Conrad Chapman is the head of a multiracial community primary school in Oldham. He was the first coordinator of the RSA's 'Home–School Contract of Partnership' Project and is currently a part-time INSET provider and lecturer at Manchester University's School of Education.

Sarah Gale is the Parent Partnership Project Manager in the London Borough of Tower Hamlets. She previously job-shared the Hackney PACT Coordinator's post with Roger Hancock who is also a contributor to this publication.

Roger Hancock et al. Roger Hancock works in the London Borough of Hackney where he coordinates the long-established project, 'Parents and children and teachers' (PACT). Currently, he is very involved in setting up a Hackney Parents' Support Service which will operate from a parents' centre. He is also an honorary research associate at the University of Greenwich.

Helen Jenner, Gavin Østmo and **Anne O'Connor** work at Harbinger School in the London Borough of Tower Hamlets. Helen is the headteacher, Gavin is a class teacher and staff development coordinator and Anne is the early years coordinator. **Geoff Sheath** is a lecturer based in the School of Primary and Secondary Education at the University of Greenwich.

Anne Houston has been Principal Project Officer with the Home School Employment Partnership in Paisley since 1991. Prior to this, she was involved in Community Education and continues to lecture part-time on the subject at Glasgow University. She has been a member of the National Home School Development Group since 1991.

Kathy Maclachlan is currently on secondment to the Department of Adult and Continuing Education at the University of Glasgow. Previously, she was the coordinator of the Partnership in Education Project in Glasgow. Her former professional experience includes work in other home/school/community projects, adult education and secondary teaching.

Ruth Merttens and Alan Newland Ruth has been a teacher for nearly 20 years and has taught all ages between 3 and 90! She was the founder of the IMPACT Project in 1985 and has lectured at the University of North London since the same date. The author of several books, including *Teaching Primary Maths* and *Bringing School Home,* she is a parent of six children whose ages range from 22 to 6 years old – this is the experience from which she has learned, and continues to learn, the most!

Alan was a deputy headteacher in Hackney and taught for fifteen years in inner London schools. He is a course tutor on a BA in Education Studies at the University of North London, and editor of the journal *Teaching Primary Studies.* Currently Alan is the co-director of the Shared Writing Project and co-author with Ruth of the book *Learning in Tandem: Parents and children learning together.*

Alwyn Morgan taught in Leicestershire schools prior to moving to Clwyd as a secondary school community tutor and later as the Community Education Coordinator for the LEA. For the past seven years he has been Humberside's School Community Officer, leading and managing the authority's substantial home–school liaison strategy, which includes a comprehensive training programme for working with parents.

Tanny Stobart is the County Coordinator for Family Education and

Playwork in Devon. For a number of years she has encouraged the development of networking and training as key ways of establishing and maintaining family education provision in some of the most rural parts of the county.

Diana Stoker is a parent educator with considerable experience of community-based projects. She has taught in Glasgow, spent two years in Algeria, and was then seconded to the Schools Council Bilingual Learners' Project. She set up ILEA's Pimlico Family Education Project in 1981 and is, at present, involved in a range of parent education projects in London primary schools.

Sheila Wolfendale has been a primary school and remedial reading teacher, an educational psychologist in several LEAs and is currently director of a Doctorate in Educational Psychology training programme at the University of East London. She has authored and edited many books, booklets, chapters, articles and handbooks on aspects of special needs, early years and parental involvement. She was awarded a Professorship in 1988 and in 1995 gained a PhD by published works.

Introduction

This book, like the series it introduces, is an attempt to capture the flavour of home–school work in Britain in the 1990s. It conveys a mixture of familiar concerns and recent developments, of shared interests and differences of approach that relate to differences of setting and circumstance. These accounts capture something of the important underlying shifts of substance and emphasis that are taking place and which constitute a new agenda. This brief introduction provides a background against which the individual contributions can be located.

The most obvious though not necessarily the most significant features of this background are the combined effects of government policy, legislation and resource allocation. Here, the key elements are the strengthening of both central government and the governing bodies of individual schools within a market system which:

- strengthens the entitlement of parents to information about the life and work of the school *and* the progress of their own children;
- gives parents and governors a clearer voice and greater influence in the management of schools;
- makes the regulation of a school's work more obviously accountable through the publication of test scores and examination results and through formal inspection.

Such influences have undeniably affected all schools, teachers and parents, although they have affected them differently.

For many hard-pressed teachers and support staff, work with parents is often viewed as something of a mixed blessing. On the positive side, most teachers now accept, however grudgingly, that there is clear and compelling evidence that greater parental interest and support leads to improved pupil achievement (Wolfendale, 1992). On a more critical note, home–school work is increasingly seen as a series of requirements and obligations, often shaped by external pressures and influences and enacted against a background of competing demands and sharply declining resources. *Not* a recipe for unconditional commitment and positive effort!

It is perhaps surprising, therefore, that home–school work, as this collection of accounts vividly testifies, continues to be an area characterised by high levels of professional energy and committed effort. For parents, these changes signal the slow but inevitable death of widespread deference, passivity and learned helplessness – although there is still a long way to go! Most parents are beginning to sense their entitlement to information, to have a say and to be listened to, even if, in reality, many still find it difficult to achieve this, and many schools do not actually encourage it. This gradual change is increasingly matched by the rising expectations of more and more parents from a wide range of backgrounds and experience, and a growing sense of being part of a shared enterprise.

Collectively, however, parents still have little or no power base, at school, local or national levels. While this is slowly changing, the efforts of a growing number and range of parent interest groups and representative organisations remain largely uncoordinated and inadequately resourced. For, in spite of the rhetoric, parents of children in the UK currently lack a clear agenda, a mandate for collective action and the political clout that is necessary to bring about genuine change (Bastiani and Doyle, 1994). Interestingly, at the time of writing, there are a number of attempts to establish such an agenda – one being the National Consumer Council's Parents' Forum – which encourage a degree of quiet optimism that important developments are taking place.

In spite of its tangible benefits and positive achievements, illustrated throughout this book, home–school work in Britain continues to be characterised by deep, intractable and problematic issues. Against a wider view, it is not difficult to see why this should be so:

> Families and schools are very different kinds of institutions. Tensions and differences are, in the real world, every bit as present as are co-operation and joint action.

> Family structure and organisation have changed profoundly over the years. Families are extremely diverse and frequently changing in complicated ways. Many families, too, are having a really hard time personally, socially and economically.

> Family–school relations, by definition, touch upon the boundaries where professional confidence and parental responsibilities meet, often exposing raw nerves on both sides. Unsurprisingly, home–school liaison calls for enormous sensitivity, special skills and experience.

> Much home–school work, in practice, can be criticised for contributing to, rather than alleviating, the growing inequalities between children and families. It does this by helping those parents who need help least and failing to reach many of those who stand to benefit most.

> Finally, family–school relations, like all major areas of education and social policy, are characterised by competing viewpoints and ideologies, widely differing experience and contradictory arguments and evidence. This applies, often with considerable force, to differences among politicians, professionals and parents.

Coming of age

Much home–school work has been sustained over many years by a combination of missionary zeal and committed, though often unself-critical, practice. In beginning to recognise the difficult nature of the work and the limitations of thinking and practice, as well as through more realistic assessment of the opportunities and constraints in our work, this collection suggests that home–school work in Britain has come of age! The following accounts attempt to illustrate in a number of ways how this is happening and what some of the consequences are.

Firstly, the arena is moving from a rather simplistic, conventional view of the main tasks to a rather sharper examination of what it is we are trying to do and what has been achieved. Most significantly, this book recognises the need to reassess the continuing usefulness of the principles upon which home–school work is currently based.

While partnership ideals have, in the past, provided an adequate focus for continuing commitment and effort, they may no longer provide an adequate basis for our changing expectations, circumstances and experience. Enthusiasm and genuineness of effort continue, of course, to be crucially important, but they may no longer be sufficient. Eventually, an honest appraisal of these shortcomings can provide a way forward for our thinking (*see* Bastiani, 1995, for a more detailed critique).

Secondly, home–school thinking and practice have, until recently, been a rather blunt instrument. They are too often undifferentiated and one-dimensional, failing to identify and respond to the range of need and experience in home–school work. Currently, there seems to be a growing awareness of the enormous range and diversity of home–school ingredients. This can and should include:

- school type, size, age range and history;
- the range of school catchment areas and social settings;
- the patterns of family, neighbourhood and community life;
- individual and group needs and circumstances among individual parents and collectively, including their own education and development.

This awareness encompasses a recognition of the importance of home–school liaison work with minority ethnic parents and families, work with parents of children with special educational needs, family literacy programmes and, more recently, work in parent education (Wolfendale, 1996). There is also a growing recognition of the need to make areas of our work part of the everyday activity of mainstream schools of all kinds, through the development of home–school policies and a whole-school approach. There is now a welcome awareness of the need to find ways of building on and extending the active support and involvement of parents as their children get older and move into secondary schools.

At the same time, ensuring the consistency and effectiveness of work with parents and others who have a responsibility for children's education, welfare and development, is now generally accepted as a key task for *all* schools and teachers. While this offers considerably enhanced opportunities, via whole-school approaches and the development of coherent policies and training, it does inevitably change the nature of the task.

Current influential work on school improvement, for example, is deeply rooted in extensive evidence from school systems around the world. This work shows clearly (e.g. Mortimore *et al.*, 1995) that the most effective schools, regardless of the age of pupils or differences in pupil entry, have certain characteristics. In every case, good quality home–school work is a key ingredient.

Above all, it is necessary to recognise the sheer *extent* of home–school work in Britain, how embedded much of it is now in the system and the depth and quality of much of its experience. Here, although progress is inevitably uneven, our work with parents has moved a few notches up the evolutionary ladder! Much of the home–school literature and practice in the past has emphasised the need to tackle long-established attitudes and obstacles and to establish new ways of working. Our concern has shifted to:

- the maintenance and further development of our work;
- issues of quality and effectiveness;
- the 'second order' problems of where we go from here!

So this collection sets out to move the agenda on from attempts to *introduce* the spread of partnership principles and practice, through attempts to implement and sustain them, to an exploration of some of the *consequences* of doing so. This is mirrored by a common theme, running not only through this book but also through the series as a whole, which recognises a growing need to:

- review what we are setting out to do and what we have achieved;
- reflect on what we have done and what can be learned from it;
- examine our own thinking in the light of our changing views and circumstances;
- identify and support promising areas of growth and development.

The content and organisation of the book

Unusually, this book has been written by members of a national group, the National Home–School Development Group (NHSDG), which has existed for nearly a decade. Its members have a special interest in and responsibility for home–school work, but through different roles and in different settings. These include the work of specially funded programmes and projects, the organisation of initiatives and development work across local education authorities (LEAs) and the study of home–school topics in advanced courses for teachers and others. The group also contains a special blend of interest and experience, exemplified by:

- home–school work throughout Britain and especially a productive mix from 'north and south of the border'!
- a commitment to the development of practitioner-based initiatives, materials and approaches;
- an active involvement in In-Service Training (INSET) and in a variety of training and development work for professionals and parents.

The NHSDG has organised a national conference to raise the profile of home–school work and to share ideas and experience. It also tackles themes of current concern, such as the place of home–school work in OFSTED inspections and the training needs generated by the new SEN Code of Practice.

The experience of group members embodies, in their respective accounts, most of the key ingredients that make home–school work such a productive mix. This includes cross-phase work in both mainstream schools and funded initiatives, adult, continuing and community education backgrounds and experience, Section 11 funded work with black and bilingual parents and also with families whose children have special educational needs.

It is hoped that continuing membership of a collaborative and mutually supportive group helps to link these aspects through the sharing of ideas and experience. The book has deliberately *not* been organised into clear, self-contained sections with designated topics, as is the convention. This is to allow maximum airing of the group's shared interests and concerns. These include:

- changing patterns of power and influence between government, LEAs and schools, and between teachers, governors, parents … and pupils;
- the need to review basic principles in the light of current experience and changing circumstances, to learn from and build on this process;
- the key importance of parental viewpoints and experience in home–school work;
- the development of effective and appropriate ways of managing change – at all levels – against a background of declining resources and competing demands.

Our accounts inevitably reflect the special preoccupations of our times. These currently include the contribution of home–school work to the raising of pupil achievement, meeting the legal requirements in this area, extending good practice to meet the needs of parents/carers of older pupils and, especially, a concern for the quality and effectiveness of a school's work with parents.

At the same time, however, contributors address a *broader* view of children's education and development. This acknowledges the importance of children's out-of-school learning in a range of family and neighbourhood settings, the significant contributions of a wide range of people and agencies and, less obvious but crucial, the need to give an airing to important viewpoints and experience that go beyond and challenge existing political and professional orthodoxies.

Finally our hope is that, taken together, these accounts suggest not only a reasonably balanced view of the satisfactions and achievements that home–school work brings, but also something of the challenges that remain and the work that has yet to be tackled.

References

Bastiani, J. (1995) *Taking a Few Risks: learning from each other; teachers, parents and pupils.* London: RSA. Available from RSA (Education), 8, John Adam Street, London WC2N 6EZ.

Bastiani, J. and Doyle, N. (1994) *Home and School: building a better partnership.* London: National Consumer Council.

Mortimore, P., Hillman, J. and Sammons, P. (1995) *Key Characteristics of Effective Schools: a review of school effectiveness research.* London: London Institute of Education (published for OFSTED).

Wolfendale, S. (1992) *Empowering Parents and Teachers – Working for Children.* London: Cassell.

Wolfendale, S. (1996) 'Enhancing Parental Effectiveness' in Sigston, A., Curran, P., Labram, A. and Wolfendale, S. (Eds) *Psychology in Practice: with young people, families and schools.* London: David Fulton.

1 Managing the changing power bases – parents, schools, governors and LEAs

Alwyn Morgan

This chapter examines the manner in which working relationships between LEAs, governing bodies, schools and parents have changed as a consequence of government legislation. Three models of accountability are examined: firstly, the traditional perspective with the LEA as the all embracing power, with parents being an after-thought for schools and governing bodies. This is followed by a description of the present transitionary position where all concerned are readjusting to either their increased or decreased powers. Finally, a third model is explored which meets with cross-party political support, that sees parents in a position hardly imaginable a generation ago.

In conclusion, the author questions this position, preferring a model of 'shared responsibility' for children's education. However, he believes that from his own practical experience, this goal will not be attained successfully unless a range of management decisions is addressed.

In recent years government legislation has brought about dramatic and rapidly imposed changes within the administration and management of education. This has called upon elected members and all education personnel to adapt their working practices in a very short period.

These changes have had an impact on four particular target groups, namely the following.

Local Education Authorities

Already the consequences of the newly imposed working practices have had marked effect on all concerned. The devolution of previously centrally held funding to schools has led to slimming down exercises, with substantially smaller numbers of personnel being employed centrally. For those remaining, the new funding arrangements are calling for imaginative and relevant 'market forces' practices and services to be employed. Additionally, the Funding Agency for Schools (FAS) established for grant-maintained schools, has cast a further shadow on this debate.

The former monolithic nature of LEAs is now history.

Schools

Many of the powers and responsibilities lost by the LEAs have been transferred to schools. While many complaints have been heard from this direction regarding the changed nature of the challenges of school management, the vast majority of headteachers have welcomed the greater control, influence and autonomy accorded to them. Moreover, this newly acquired freedom has spurred many heads and their governing bodies to discard the overriding mantle of the LEA altogether and seek grant-maintained status.

Governing bodies

Historically, school governing bodies have had token management oversight for the well-being of schools. Power and responsibilities were limited, with overall accountability being to the LEA. Over and above such constraints, it is generally accepted that the headteacher, in consultation with the chair of the governing body, ensured that important management issues were addressed from one meeting to another.

However, as the power and influence of LEAs has waned, governing bodies have increasingly been expected to shoulder an ever-increasing workload. Governors are now expected to take decisions that would never have been expected of them a few years ago. In response to these developments training courses have become a further demand on governor time and goodwill.

Parents

Until recently many schools and LEAs regarded parents very much as a peripheral issue. They were considered as one of the least of the schools' priorities for action or staff training. They were certainly not a priority for funding, involvement or provision of information. Additionally, there was only minimal formal acknowledgement for their potential to contribute to raising standards of attainment. Dialogue with parents was limited on account of the professional's view that 'they wouldn't understand anyway'. However, in order to gain an insight into how recent government legislation has changed the power bases within education today, it may be helpful to refer to Figure 1.1, outlining what the author considers to be the:

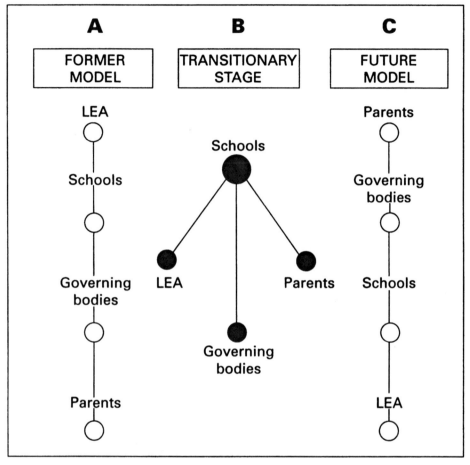

Figure 1.1 Changing times, roles and responsibilities

- former power model
- current transitionary phase
- developing power model.

The former power model

It will be noted from Figure 1.1 and earlier comments, that in the traditional model the LEA was the all-embracing power in the administration and management of education. Few decisions could be questioned.

Below the LEA were schools, with many heads having the potential to direct both their governing bodies and parents with autocratic authority. Governor and parental involvement with schools was somewhat limited.

Governing bodies were generally regarded as 'rubber-stamping' the headteacher and chairperson's decisions. Few governors were known to either teaching staff or parents.

Parents were infrequently consulted on school policy issues. Schools that actively encouraged an effective dialogue with parents were certainly in the minority. Generally speaking, the role and importance of parents was rarely given the acknowledgement it deserved. Many parents recall not being allowed nearer the school than the school gate or beyond a white line drawn across the school yard.

The transitionary phase

The government-instigated process of change has generated a constant state of managerial flux within the system, with all interested parties vying, almost in chess-like fashion, for power, influence and control. The current state of play is that the schools are in the ascendancy, while the role of the LEA is diminishing, and increasingly becoming a subject of debate. This is acknowledged in the Labour Party education policy statement entitled *Diversity and Excellence*, which states that: 'The whole notion of LEA control of schools – on which the drive for GM status was started – is a thing of the past. LEAs do not control schools. Schools do' (1995: 1).

While acknowledging that many LEA powers have been devolved to school governing bodies, there is still considerable frustration felt by many governors, particularly parent governors, that headteachers are finding it difficult to devolve full democratic powers to the governing body. School management tensions are now becoming apparent and are frequently reported in the *Times Education Supplement*. Typical headlines include 'Number of heads suspended doubles' (9.6.95) and 'Over-trained, over-keen and finally, overruled' (23.6.95).

Additionally, it is also fair to surmise that generally speaking parents have yet to appreciate the influence that they can bring to bear upon schools. While the 'professional' may reluctantly acknowledge that because of the new funding arrangement for schools, parents are now clients, the vast majority of parents have either yet to see themselves in such a role or to be treated accordingly.

Furthermore, because of the parental consultation process attached to OFSTED inspections, schools should now also regard parents as consultants on their work.

Consequently, at the present time, some major accountability changes are being brought about within the education sector, the implications of which are not fully appreciated or acted upon in a serious manner by the key players.

The developing power model

For how long this transitionary stage will continue is uncertain. The government wishes to see parents exercising their choice of school in order to influence the nature and quality of educational provision. Consequently, if and when parents appreciate and act on the full potential of their role, a complete inversion of power, influence and control will have taken place, as noted in Figure 1.1. Parents will have moved from being a peripheral issue into the pole position, while LEAs may be left to examine a role more appropriate to current or future needs.

The accountability of schools to parents is currently an issue that appears to have cross-party political support. The Dearing Report stated that: 'Schools have a fundamental responsibility for the future well-being of our nation. They must, therefore, be accountable to parents and society as a whole. I believe teachers accept this' (Dearing, 1993: para. 3.35). This issue appears to be given even greater significance in 'Diversity and excellence'. Included in the four principles that govern Labour's approach to the organisation of schooling is the following statement: 'accountability must exist locally to parents and the community as well as nationally to central government' (Labour Party, 1995: 1). This is a major issue that requires debate by both governors and teachers alike.

Prior to concluding this section, it may be desirable to question whether all concerned wish to see this summarised model becoming the driving force behind educational provision. There will obviously be varying views on this matter. The author of this chapter offers an alternative model (Figure 1.2) for consideration, that while acknowledging that schools need to be accountable for their performance, there is a need for all concerned to work together to share the responsibility for young people's education. Much has been talked about partnerships in children's education (which this model purports), but unfortunately in the past, the reality has not matched the rhetoric. Nevertheless, this should be the goal that parents, schools and their governing bodies should work for.

The leadership, expertise, coordination and guidance provided by LEAs over the years should not be disregarded. *Diversity and Excellence* summarises the role of the LEA as: 'The job of the LEA is to support schools in identifying good practice and spreading it and in identifying weakness and rooting it out' (Labour Party, 1995: 14). The collective expertise and goodwill of all parties concerned is essential in harnessing a climate in which all pupils can be encouraged to maximise on their true potential. Effective and harmonious working relationships between the respective bodies should therefore be a pre-requisite for coordinating the complementary expertise that enhances the quality of education provision.

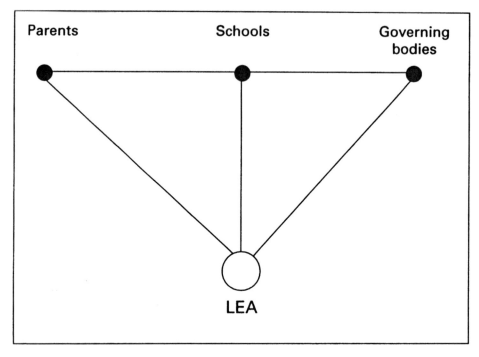

Figure 1.2 Sharing the responsibility for children's education

The management challenge

The above goal will not be achieved easily. It will therefore be very necessary for schools, their governing bodies and LEAs to consider their position relating to parents.

The following points are offered for consideration. They are merely a personal reflection based on considerable first-hand experience of the home–school scene. There are probably other responses which will also be called for.

1 There needs to be a positive acceptance by all concerned that the power bases within education have changed and that parents should be fully acknowledged as co-educators of their children, as well as clients and consultants on the educational service.

2 LEAs, governors and teachers need to undertake an audit of their respective establishments to review their current level of interaction with parents. This may demonstrate where parents feature within their organisation's priorities.

3 Having completed such an exercise it would then be prudent for parent and client/consultant services to be placed as a regular item on the meeting agendas for schools and LEAs. Only rarely in the past have

parents featured as an issue for discussion by governing bodies, teachers or education committees. Can parents, in this new market-forces climate be treated with such disregard?

4 In order to reflect the current situation, all schools and LEAs require a well thought through parent/client policy statement, and identified goals to be worked towards in the development plans.

5 This new climate of accountability to clients will call upon a greater level of accessibility of governors and LEAs. The Labour Party proposals for LEAs to 'make further progress in developing their new role as the champions of parents and their communities', allied to the requirement for parent forums (1995: 14), holds some promise. Accessibility of governors is an issue that has long been unresolved.

6 The developing role of parents will undoubtedly demand that resources are earmarked for this work. Unfortunately in the past this has not been readily forthcoming. For the average school and LEA, funding for work with parents has been relatively minuscule. A comparison with the business sector demonstrates that market research and customer services demands a healthy percentage of any business budget, which in turn brings its return in revenue and goodwill. This is an issue that all concerned in the educational service will need to address, even within the constraints of shrinking budgets.

7 The immediate resource consideration is funding and provision of training. Few educational personnel have been trained to work with parents and this consequently may account for the low status accorded to parents. There is an urgent need to rectify this situation.

8 The changing times require all teachers and LEA workers to examine and act upon the parental dimension of their respective roles. However, there is also a need to allocate specific posts and sufficient time for people to lead, coordinate and develop effective liaison with parents.

9 Finally, the author believes that radical, imaginative and collaborative responses will be called for if all concerned are to make a reality of the 'shared responsibility' for children's education. Yesteryears' working practices may not be the solutions for the new working relationships that need to be addressed.

Can or should this challenge be ignored?

References

Dearing, R. (1993) *The National Curriculum and its Assessment*, December. London: School Curriculum and Assessment Authority.

14

Labour Party (1995) *Diversity and Excellence – a new partnership for schools.* London: Labour Party.

Times Education Supplement (9.6.95) *Number of heads suspended doubles,* Rafferty, F., No. 4119, p. 1.

Times Education Supplement (23.6.95) *Over-trained, over-keen and finally, overruled,* No. 4121, p. 13.

2 Learning begins at home: implications for a learning society

Titus Alexander

Imagine an education system where none of the educators is trained, indeed, where training is seen as a sign of weakness. There is no curriculum, but the amount to be learnt is vast and it is assumed everyone knows what it is. There is no assessment, but if people fail the penalties are severe. This is not any old education system, but the foundation for every course, job and profession in the country. It is, of course, the family. Parents are the most important educator in any person's life, yet they get most of the blame when things go wrong and the least support and training to ensure that all children get the best possible start in life.

As knowledge, skills and interpersonal competence become increasingly important for employment and other opportunities throughout life, so the importance of this foundation course in life is likely to grow. Thus concern for equality of opportunity as well as attainment demands that the education system takes account of children's different starting points and home circumstances.

It would be quite wrong to 'professionalise' parenting through training, assessment and qualifications and thus increase the pressures on parents. But the formal education system needs to do much more to recognise and support families' fundamental role as the foundation for all learning.

Learning within the family is more lasting and influential than any other. Values, attitudes, behaviour, language and a vast range of skills are learnt or shaped at home. Family life can be a source of inspiration and personal growth, stimulating learning throughout life. But family experiences can – and often do – cause stress, distress and even illness, damaging personal development and inhibiting learning.

Experiences within the family have a profound influence on peoples' learning and life chances. Many studies show that home background is the most single significant factor in educational achievement at school and in later life (e.g. Bloom, 1985). Poor parenting is associated with low achievement and even criminality in later life (Utting, 1995). Where there is abuse, conflict or neglect, or parents/carers are stressed, depressed and unable to cope, family life can cause terrible suffering, permanent damage and long-term disadvantage.

Family life is not a happy experience for many people. A survey by NCH

Action for Children suggests that at least 750,000 children in Britain suffer long-term trauma as a result of domestic violence (NCH Action for Children, 1994). Over 36,000 children are on the Child Protection Register. Over 7,000 cases of sexual abuse were reported in 1992. It is estimated that one in eight adults were beaten or abused as children. The numbers who suffered from constant criticism or emotional neglect are much greater. Millions of people seek help from counsellors, therapists or the Samaritans, or suffer from mental illness, often tracing their distress to experiences within the family. Virtually all parents want the very best for their children, and indeed do their best. But when abuse, neglect or even just a lack of love is their only education in family life, the best they can offer their own children may be not be enough.

Raising children is an act of love and a source of joy. Most families are 'good enough'. But the pressures on parents have certainly increased over the past 25 years, family patterns have changed significantly and past experience is no an longer adequate guide to the future. On present trends, a quarter of children born today will see their parents divorce before they are sixteen years old. Although eight out of ten families with dependent children have two parents, some 8 per cent of children have a step-parent and a fifth of all families are headed by a lone parent, usually the mother. Two-thirds of all mothers have jobs and families are increasingly divided between 'dual earner' families and homes where nobody has a paid job (Utting, 1995). Families are also much more mobile and less likely to live close to relatives. Britain is also more ethnically diverse, with a greater variety of home languages, faiths, cultures and family patterns. The amount of information and entertainment available in many homes through the media and computer technologies has increased enormously. At the same time, the divide between families has also grown wider, in both material and educational resources.

An early challenge facing any new parent is learning to deal with a bewildering patchwork of provision, from antenatal services and health visitors to an ever-changing voluntary sector of playgroups, one-o'clock clubs, toy libraries and the arcane enrolment criteria of different nurseries. This experience rarely inspires people in their own competence. It usually generates anxiety, defensiveness or sheer exhaustion. And in the middle of all this, people somehow learn to be parents, the most important job in the world.

Families experiencing difficulties often do not know where to turn. Asking for help sounds like failure, an admission that you cannot cope. Many are afraid of interfering officialdom and the risk that their child may be taken away. Parents brave – or desperate – enough to overcome these fears must find their way round a maze of services lacking coherence and coordination. Agencies like health and social services, and the police are also beginning to recognise the need to work together in dealing with family problems, although most are far from doing so. According to a 1994 Audit Commission report, agencies set up to support children and families, which cost £2 bn a year, are badly coordinated, poorly focused and did not involve parents sufficiently (Audit Commission, 1994).

The education system is the biggest warren in this maze. It has little to offer people as parents. A lucky few discussed relationships and parent-hood, awkwardly perhaps, on the fringes of sex education. Then there may be a part-time play group or nursery as the child grows. But there are no opportunities for the adult to come to terms with the experience of becoming a parent. And when nursery or school begins, however friendly and welcoming, the overwhelming emphasis is on the parent as a vehicle for the child and on maintaining the institutional routine.

Growing numbers of schools recognise the value of working in partnership with parents, which in practice usually means the mother. But most of the emphasis is on involving parents in school, in teaching parents to extend school work. Home-learning schemes, like PACT (reading) and IMPACT (maths), are about taking school home. Relatively little attention has been given to bringing experience from home and community into school, or using the school as a resource centre for supporting the home as a place of learning.

It would be more productive if schools and other services saw their main job as providing professional support for families and the community to solve problems themselves in order to prevent them from becoming crises. This would mean designing services round families' needs for learning and support, rather than expecting families to fit in with the institutional needs of education and the caring professions. We need to turn schools round, not just in terms of the kind of activity and curriculum offered, but also who schools are for. Much more emphasis needs to be put on giving parents opportunities to learn, with their children as well as in their own right.

I want to suggest that the education system can only become learner centred by fully recognising that the home is the most significant place of learning in peoples' lives. Teachers, schools, libraries and other services provide vital resources to children and families, but the way in which they are provided makes all the difference. Our failure to do this means that most educational resources, including teachers' time, are probably wasted.

The wasting education system

Most educational provision is wasted because it is not organised to support learning as and when the learner is best able to make use of it, but to a predetermined pattern based on historical habit more than a conscious design for learning. This pattern includes long summer holidays so that children can help their parents bring in the harvest. The school year starts in the autumn with exams in the summer, like an old-fashioned assembly line, although we know that this disadvantages children born at the 'wrong' time of year. Class sizes remain remarkably constant throughout the day and over a year, although we know that learning needs everything from one-to-one coaching to very large groups, as well as work in pairs and groups without a teacher. School buildings are closed to learning for more than three-quarters of the time. Of course there are exceptions, particularly in community schools, but this ancient pattern is the basis of all funding, training and administration for education in the 21st century.

We know that educational resources are being wasted because young people, endowed with an innate capacity to learn, achieve far less than their full potential by the time they leave school. We know from our own experience, if not from school inspections, that almost a third of all lessons are unsatisfactory. That is an awful lot of wasted time for pupils, teachers and educational plant. Most lessons are satisfactory, but few are memorable moments of learning. We know that even children who appear to do well at school are simply learning to survive and play the school game successfully and cannot apply what they appear to know to their own lives because it is divorced from their lives. It is, therefore, not surprising that so many young people go on to further education without really knowing what they want to do. Many leave courses before finishing them or choose qualifications and careers they later regret.

This wastage is compounded by the high cost of juvenile crime, children in care and other services needed to cope with the large numbers of people who leave school ill-equipped to lead satisfying, healthy lives and get involved with crime, drugs or other forms of abuse. Crime alone costs the country over £18 billion a year, more than enough to double spending on education. Poverty and lack of opportunities for young people leaving school are a significant factor in these problems, but they are not the cause. Many children from poor and deprived homes do not commit crime or become abusive adults. We know that the quality of relationships within the home is one of the biggest influences on people's ability to make the most of whatever circumstances they face in life and to overcome poverty and deprivation. This is the experience of many immigrant families, into Britain, the United States and other countries, who arrived with nothing.

Educational resources are wasted, above all, because they do not acknowledge or support the vast range of independent learning that goes on at home and in the community. Children are in school for only a small proportion of waking time between birth and the age of sixteen – less than 15 per cent. Yet educational provision is planned as if it alone were the source of all knowledge. Relatively little attention is paid to the vast range of abilities among children when they come to school, even though we know that range of ability remains unchanged unless the less able get extra help as early as possible. In most schools there is very little constructive communication between teachers and the most important educators in a child's life, their parents. Most direct communication between home and school concerns administrative matters or instructions from the school to parents, about what they should do, about how the school sees their child and about things that have gone wrong.

This waste of educational resources is endemic and systemic. It is not the fault of individual teachers or even schools. Although many schools and teachers could improve their contribution to learning, even the most ambitious, well-financed school improvement programme cannot address the chronic weakness of our educational system until it stops neglecting its foundations: families as places of learning.

Effective families are fun

'It takes a whole village to educate a child' goes the African proverb. This is still true in the fast moving world of a global village, where events in Guangdong, Seattle or Wall Street can have more impact on our lives than our neighbourhood, town hall or even parliament. Multimedia, television and computer technologies can bring more information and knowledge into people's homes today than most universities held in the past. But what they do not bring is the guide, the skilled facilitator and teacher which enables people to direct their learning and create their own coherent understanding of the world.

Instead, children learn to live in a fragmented world of separate realities among fleeting television characters, heroes of the football pitch, the strange order of school and jumble of home life. Families are so very varied it is difficult to generalise, but whether a child's family is chaotic and dangerous or loving and safe, it is the most constant reality for almost all children. Even a child that is moved incessantly between relatives, childminders and a series of temporary homes, including council care, usually has a mother, grandmother or other family figure holding some kind of thread more lasting than any school.

Family experience, however secure or disturbed, is the foundation of a child's learning throughout life. Many studies have shown the contribution parents make to children's learning (e.g. Minns, 1990; Hancock, 1995; Hannon et al., 1991). In *The Meaning Makers,* Gordon Wells shows 'the very strong relationship between knowledge of literacy at age five and all later assessments of school achievement' (Wells, 1986). Barbara Tizard and Martin Hughes's study of four-year-old girls at home and in school showed that 'the home provides a very powerful learning environment' covering a very wide range of topics (Tizard and Hughes, 1984). From their detailed observations, it was clear that interactions between mothers and children at home were richer learning experiences than those with teachers. The nursery school usually offered more resources, opportunities to play with other children and other activities which provided different learning experiences not available at home, so the authors did not argue that schools were unnecessary, but that they should take account of home learning and the gap between home and school. Their study also highlighted important differences in the way in which working and middle-class children interacted with school, and the extent to which working-class parents undervalued their contribution to their child's learning.

Tizard and Hughes conclude by summarising five factors which make the home such a varied and effective learning context. These are:

1 the extensive range of activities within or from home, links with the wider world through parents' work, shopping and other activities, and the models of adults engaged with life;

2 the vast body of shared experience which enables the parent, usually the mother, to help the child make sense of experience and put it into a framework of knowledge;

3 the opportunities for sustained one-to-one conversations and undivided attention are much greater where the ratio of adults to children is so much smaller than in school;

4 learning is embedded in contexts of great meaning, where the outcome has emotional and practical importance;

5 the intimacy and intensity of home can give children greater freedom and safety to pursue questions, while the mother's concern for the child means she will put whatever energy she has into pursuing her educational expectations for her child.

'It is this parental concern that converts the potential advantages of the home into actual advantages', the authors continue. 'The learning potential of the home is not a necessary attribute of all family settings' (Tizard and Hughes, 1984).

The authors criticise home-visiting schemes and most parent education courses, questioning 'the assumption that professionals know how parents should interact with, and educate, their children'. They conclude that there is a 'useful role for parents' groups, and for advice and information centres which respond to these needs [for sharing experiences, support and learning], but none for attempts by professionals to alter the way in which parents carry out their educational role'. 'Indeed, in our opinion, it is time to shift the emphasis away from what parents should learn from professionals and towards what professionals can learn from studying parents and children at home' (Tizard and Hughes, 1984).

There is little evidence that schools and professionals have made a significant shift towards learning from parents and children at home. The development of home–school links, as documented in this book and elsewhere (RSA, 1993), shows that recognition of the importance of parents is widespread, but the full implications of this and other studies have not been assimilated by the education system or policy-makers.

Yet there has been growth in different kinds of parenting education in response to parents' needs. These courses or parents groups provide opportunities to share experiences and learn practical strategies for dealing with everyday problems. Programmes like *Parent Link* and *Family Caring Trust* are not run by professional agencies, but by parents or volunteers who have trained to use parents' own experiences and a package of materials with groups. Unlike the professional parent education courses criticised by Tizard and Hughes, which are mainly targeted at parents considered 'deprived' or 'inadequate', these courses are more available in middle-class areas where parents can afford to pay. These parents see the value of improving parenting and are less likely to fear intervention by social services or other professionals than in many poor areas. But many of these materials are also being used successfully by working-class, African Caribbean and bilingual Asian parents, as in the London Borough of Waltham Forest.

The National Children's Bureau's comprehensive survey of policy and practice in parent education in 1994 listed the main features of these programmes (Pugh *et al.*, 1994). This describes an emerging 'pedagogy of family' which is also relevant to schools. Among the key points are:

- a belief that 'good enough' parents are responsible, authoritative, assertive, positive, democratic and consistent;
- they are not autocratic, authoritarian or permissive;
- parents' strengths should be reaffirmed, building on confidence and self-esteem;
- experience, feelings and relationships are as important as knowledge, with the emphasis on understanding and enjoyment.

This pedagogy is consistent with over a decade of research into well-motivated high achievers from low-income backgrounds in the United States, from which Reginald Clark concluded that 'effective families' had made the biggest difference in children's lives:

Like effective schools, effective families have a set of easy-to-identify characteristics. These cut across family income, education, and ethnic background. They remain true for single- and two-parent households and for families with working and non-working mothers. Effective families display a number of positive attitudes and behaviours towards their children which help them to succeed in school and in life. (Clark, 1983; 1987)

The characteristics of effective families also describe a pedagogy of family learning from which educational professionals could learn:

1 *a feeling of control over their lives:* parents believe they can make a positive difference in their children's lives and do not feel overwhelmed by circumstances. Their homes are a safe place for children to find support and understanding;

2 *frequent communication of high expectations;*

3 *a family dream of success for the future:* parents have a vision of success for each child and talk with their children about the steps to realise them;

4 *a view of hard work as a key to success;*

5 *an active lifestyle:* parents encourage children to use out-of-school activities and community resources, they know where their children are, who they are with and encourage them to associate with children who have similar values regarding work and school;

6 *25 to 35 home-centred learning hours a week:* including homework, reading, hobbies, household chores, family outings and youth programmes;

7 *the family as a mutual support system* in which parents give children some appropriate responsibilities from an early age and children realise they are needed and contribute to family life;

8 *clearly understood household rules, consistently enforced,* with the emphasis on acceptance and responsibility rather than punishment;

9 *frequent contact with teachers* and involvement in school life;

10 *emphasis on spiritual growth,* encouraging children to find inner peace and love.

The most significant feature of these ten points is that they are based on a study of successful young adults from poor, black families. They bear the hallmarks of their particular culture and society, but many are relevant to the British education system.

The central point is that we know many of the features which contribute to family failure, we know the general characteristics of effective families, and we know what kind of education and support for parents can make a positive contribution to their role as educators, yet none of this is recognised in the education system.

It has been said that, on average, people learn half of everything they are taught during their lives during the first five years. It is probably impossible to quantify and compare learning in this way, but it is certain that we could not do without everything we learn by the age of five, and those skills, knowledge and abilities we acquire by the age of six make all the different to all subsequent learning. It would therefore make sense to secure adequate resources and support for those vital early years. What might this mean in practice?

A vision of a learning society

A learning society would be one in which, above all else, parents and other family members had time to spend with children. Work, wages and welfare would be structured in such a way that parents could choose to spend significant amounts of time with their children, particularly in the early years, without being penalised financially. Family income support, maternity/paternity leave and services for people with dependent children would be recognised as an investment in education, not a cost to be cut by getting parents into employment as quickly as possible. Increased opportunities for women to work would be matched by more opportunities for fathers to spend time with their children. Family-friendly policies by employers are not just good personnel practice, but a vital part of training and staff development for future generations.

Secondly, families would have a wide choice of affordable activities, courses and provision to support and extend learning in the home, starting with antenatal classes and continuing through to intergenerational activities with older people and bereavement counselling. Parenting education would be a small but significant part of total provision, and most parents would expect to participate in some kind of support group, parenting programme or activity to develop their abilities as parents. It would be quite normal and easy for parents to seek advice and support for any concerns when they arise.

Thirdly, every school and public library would be a community education centre, open every day for most of the year, providing resources and support for learning to all family members, as and when they wanted to learn. Grandparents and other adults would be actively involved. School premises would be a focus for community celebrations and neighbourhood democracy as well as places of learning.

The process of attending school would be turned inside out, as is beginning in a very few places. There would be huge encouragement and incentives for parents and children to participate in activities and a nursery or playgroup before school age. Children would start classes at school when they were ready and able to learn in class. School would start with parents, teacher and child making a joint assessment of what the child could do and what she could best learn next. The exercise would be repeated every term. A group of children would spend much of the time together as a class with a teacher, but the variety of activities and adults in class would be greater. The ratio of children to a class teacher would rise from about 8:1 in infant school to 20:1 in secondary, but there would be more variety in group sizes for different activities and specialist subjects. The average ratio across the school system might even be similar to now, but there would be many more teachers in early years and more self-directed study groups and projects at secondary level. Lessons would draw on children's experience and activities outside school much more, including television, film, hobbies and excursions. Young people would take work home to apply and practise what they have learnt in school, and bring experiences into school in order to understand and engage with the world in which they are growing up.

Teachers and parents would meet at least once every half term in a class meeting to discuss the curriculum, progress and anything affecting the class as a whole. All parents would meet the teacher for an in-depth discussion at least once every term. Many parents, family members and other adults would spend more time in school, sharing their experience and knowledge, helping out and learning themselves. Continuity of experience between home and school would flow both ways, with school more like the intimate, interactive meaningful personal learning that takes place in most homes, while the range of knowledge, skills and issues developed at home would deepen.

The functions of home and school would still be distinct, perhaps even more so than today. With a clear partnership between home and school, teachers of skills and knowledge could be confident that child and parents will expect to learn at home. Whole-class teaching might be more widespread than now, because lessons would be focused on what participants were ready and willing to learn and there would be a lot more small group learning in people's lives beyond the classroom.

School would not be seen as the source or store of knowledge, but a place where people could develop their skills and deepen their understanding of the knowledge that is all around them. Children and parents would bring questions and problems to learn about in school, and all would work together at the frontiers of knowledge in the 21st century.

Schools cannot make this transformation alone. Children and parents already bring many problems to school which act as a block to learning. In order to create a learning society we need to recognise and transform the educational role of *every* agency that works with families.

Learning beyond school

Recognising that home is the centre of life and learning also means reorganising the way in which many public services are provided. From the public's point of view, services for families and children are a bewildering maze. Finding the help or advice you need can be a hazardous voyage of chance and frustration. Trying to influence service providers is even more difficult, since they are answerable to different branches of government or voluntary organisation, each pursuing a different agenda according to different timetables. Getting agencies to develop a comprehensive strategy together is extremely difficult.

There are few examples where agencies have really transformed the way they work together to put families first. In many areas early years networks link playgroup workers, nursery nurses, teachers, education visitors and others at a local level. They are often informal, meeting in lunch breaks to share information and support. The 1989 Children Act has increased coordination of provision for under-eights, with some joint planning between education, social services, health and sometimes other agencies. But joint planning is still subject to departmental priorities. Since every department has different priorities and different funding criteria, progress is slow and is just as likely to be in reverse as moving forward.

The only example I know of a serious attempt to coordinate family services is in Washington State, USA. The legislature has set up a state-wide Family Policy Council on which all agencies that work with families are represented, from education and health to the juvenile justice system, together with elected representatives. This structure is reproduced at local level. Every county of about 40,000 people has a Community Network of 23 people, ten from the different agencies and thirteen representing different community interests. The Council and each Network has a responsibility to plan provision for the area. They have powers to vary departmental funding criteria, so that funds can be allocated flexibly to meet specific needs of the area. The Family Policy Council and Networks were set up as a preventative strategy in response to rising juvenile crime, drug use and children at risk, but their scope is wide, including recreation and creativity. These 'policy-focused networks' aim to cut across departmental boundaries and develop joint strategies for all agencies which work with families, and to give users more direct access to strategic decision-making. Breaking down the hierarchies and functional barriers between institutions set up to serve families is as important as turning schools inside out.

Schools are a vital element of this strategy, as a community focus in contact with most families and young people in the neighbourhood. Schools bring together people from different faiths, denominations and,

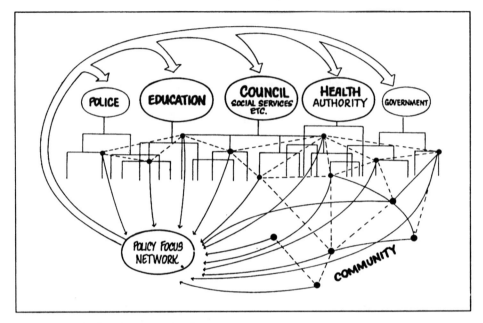

Figure 2.1 Policy focus network

quite often, different social backgrounds and ethnic origins. Schools are potential successors to places of worship as a focus for community life, in which community values, experience and knowledge can be shared. The emphasis on parental choice and competition between schools increases community fragmentation, valuing division over cohesion. The potential of schools as a meeting place for shared learning as well as social events and political action remains a vital part of the vision. But at its centre are families as the foundation for learning throughout life. We ignore the enduring centrality of home at our peril. Home is, in every sense, the very heart of learning.

References

Audit Commission (1994) *Seen But Not Heard: co-ordinating community child health and social services for children in need.* London: HMSO.

Bloom, B.S. (1985) *Developing Talent in Young People.* New York: Ballantine.

Clark, R.M. (1983) *Family Life and School Achievement: why poor black children succeed or fail.* Chicago: University of Chicago Press.

Clark, R.M. (1987) 'Effective Families Help Children Succeed in School', *Network for Public Schools,* 1. Columbia, USA: National Committee for Citizens in Education.

Hancock, R. (1995) 'Family Literacy: a French connection', *Primary Teaching Studies,* 9(1), Spring.

Hannon, P.L., Weinberger, J. and Nutbrown, C. (1991) 'A Study of Work with Parents to Promote Early Literacy Development', *Research Papers in Education*, 6: 77–97.

Minns, H. (1990) *Read it to me now! Learning at home and at school*. London: Virago.

NCH Action for Children (1994) *The Hidden Victims – Children and Domestic Violence*. London: NCH Action for Children.

Pugh, G., De'Ath, E. and Smith, C. (1994) *Confident Parents, Confident Children: policy and practice in parent education and support*. London: National Children's Bureau, pp. 76–7.

RSA (1993) *Directory of Home–School Initiatives*. London: RSA.

Tizard, B. and Hughes, M. (1984) *Young Children Learning: talking and thinking at home and at school*. London: Fontana.

Utting, D. (1995) *Family and Parenthood: supporting families, preventing breakdown*. York: Joseph Rowntree Foundation.

Wells, G. (1986) *The Meaning Makers*. London: Hodder and Stoughton.

3 Good mothers are women too: the gender implications of parental involvement in education

Kathy Maclachlan

Many of the women here (an estate in Glasgow) they've not got the confidence ... and it's a shame, but I think it all stems back from school. You see, like me when I was going through school, you think – you just come here and get through the day and that's it, and it's not till years later that you think, God what a mug I was, what a fool. If I'd have had my mother as involved in school, that would've helped me. But you didn't have it. No, the teacher wouldn't have wanted them there then, and it would've made a difference.

(Marie, a Glasgow mother)

Introduction

In less than the generation referred to by this mother, parental involvement in education has mushroomed and shifted from the radical margins of experimental education to the expected norms of mainstream practice. This sometimes quiet but always significant revolution, drawing parents increasingly into the centre and the management of the educational experience has the potential to effect enormous change in the lives of those it touches, change that can be to their advantage, but that can also be discriminatory in ways that have barely begun to be unravelled. And while key players in the field have, of necessity, focused their efforts on extending the practice of parental involvement and justifying its worth, this gargantuan persuasive exercise has understandably found little space for fundamental critical analysis which could shake the recently cemented foundations upon which the work has grown.

While not wishing to undermine these foundations, or even deny the undoubtable benefits that parental involvement produces, I will offer in this chapter a critical look at one particular aspect of the work, and suggest that perhaps it should be accompanied by the equivalent of a health warning to parents, a warning whose message would read, 'Can cause harm to you as a woman'.

For as schools are inexorably drawn into the educational quasi-market, where quantitative criteria, exam passes, attendance rates, ratios and parental programmes are increasingly used to sell schools to their potential customers, there is a real danger that notions of value and consequence are subsumed in the race for numerical supremacy. And paradoxically because parental involvement, if not parental partnership, is now so commonplace in schools (David, 1993; Wolfendale, 1992), and because it is assumed to benefit those concerned (Bastiani, 1993), pragmatic considerations of ways and means dominate much of the debate at the level of the local authority and the school, at the expense of issues of ideology and equality.

It is not my intent to challenge the demonstrable positive effects, or to question the basic validity of this work, but rather to raise a range of issues concerning parental practices which have evolved in institutions whose rules, traditions and procedures unintentionally perpetuate gender discrimination.

Encouraged by the works of Walkerdine and Lucey (1989) David *et al.* (1993) and David (1993), I undertook a small research study based in Glasgow which sought to examine the relationship between the growth of parental involvement in education, and the mothering role. It emerged from a growing concern of mine as a practitioner in the field, that increasing pressure upon women to become more formally involved in their children's education is both reinforcing and redefining the traditional role of mother as carer in a way that is potentially antithetical to the changing reality of the lives of many mothers, and in a way that actively discriminates against particular groups of women.

For given the gendered nature of parenting in British society, current parental involvement practices inevitably affect mothers more than they affect fathers, yet educational policy and practice in the field of home–school relations have rarely, if ever, taken gender into account, neither have they taken into account the many changes that have occurred in families or family life. They do, however, make very definite, if not explicit assumptions about the role and responsibilities of mothers in relation to their children's education. These assumptions, I believe, place increasing pressure upon mothers as educators in the home, and volunteer helpers in the school at a time of increasing maternal employment and family change. Furthermore they give little recognition to women as 'other than mother', as people whose non-mothering roles contribute as significantly to their children's upbringing as the more traditional caring/educating roles do. David maintains that 'there has been implicit rather than explicit gender differentiation in the strategic developments around parental involvement' (1993: 158) which, she says, focuses primarily on the 'correct' role of mothers in relation to their children's development.

I attempted therefore to examine the messages that parental

participation was sending to women as mothers, by talking to a number of mothers and headteachers, and locating their responses within the context of a feminist critique of home–school relations.

A feminist critique

Recent feminist analyses confirmed my anxieties that parental involvement may be regulating women as mothers against the best intentions of the teachers concerned. In particular, the dual emphasis on bringing parents into the school, and schools into the home, sends clear if unspoken messages to parents, particularly mothers, about certain parenting practices. They are, however, premised on a range of normatively defined interactions or relationships between mothers and children (Walkerdine and Lucey, 1989; Phoenix *et al.*, 1991) which assume the presence of a wide range of specific teaching and learning strategies within the home that are adopted by the 'good' sensitive mother. Walkerdine and Lucey, in describing these 'invisible pedagogues' comment:

> No longer can we differentiate between the physical tasks which make up women's housework and the work of mothering. The two are the same. Housework can no longer simply be seen as physical 'valueless' drudgery ... women's domestic labour has become the basis of modern ideas about how children learn, and housework, in its metamorphosis has become integral to the function of sensitive mothering.
>
> (1989: 68)

They suggest that the door to educational success can be opened by parents (mothers) if they have the knowledge, time and inclination to mother in certain specified ways that have demonstrably benefited certain groups of children within the existing system. So classes, groups and programmes flourish to teach those not already in the know, the skills of 'good' mothering. 'The whole discourse of parental involvement assumes that teachers must teach parents (almost always mothers) how to prepare and help their children in the right ways' (Walkerdine and Lucey, 1989: 181). Furthermore the reality of much parental involvement assumes that mothers will be available to participate as either informal teachers or volunteer helpers, and that this participation is what mothers themselves want, whether they realise it or not. Scott (1990) highlighted this issue in her survey of pre-school parental involvement in Strathclyde, Scotland:

> Modern educational politics has not as yet addressed the problems here – the impact of different family experience or demands, and the conflicting attitudes towards provision on offer. Instead the usual response has been merely to acknowledge that not everyone wishes to, or can be, involved, whilst at the

same time, predicating provision on the assumption that all good mothers should really want such involvement and be able to participate.

(1990: 6)

This powerful, stereotypical image of the 'good' mother–child relationship acts as an agent of women's oppression in sustaining the belief that mothers belong primarily in the home as educators of their children, where their main function is in producing the optimum environment for growth and development, as defined by others and whether they like it or not. So in promoting an 'acceptable' model of mothering, parental involvement inevitably impacts upon mothers and families. It validates and therefore reinforces traditional norms which locate the mother/educator in the home; it exerts pressure to become involved for the good of the child, potentially limiting mothers' activities in the public world; it discriminates against women whose lives do not conform to this pattern, and by default therefore it fails to affirm women's non-mothering roles. Phoenix, in Phoenix *et al.* (1991), suggests that the 'motherhood mandate' which incorporates certain types of relationships with children and schools permits maternal employment as long as it does not take precedence over motherhood.

The more schools demand of parents (mothers), the greater the reinforcement of these traditional, oppressive ideals which not only fail to recognise family change and the significant growth in women's employment, but also penalise those mothers who do not accord with the idealised model, through implicit censure or through exclusion. Lareau comments:

We believe that there must be a restructuring of family/school relations to reflect the changes occurring both within school and the larger society … Teacher's expectations for parental participation in schooling have escalated in the last few decades, precisely at the same time that changes in family structures have reduced familial resources for participating in schooling.

(1989: 254)

The study

Bearing in mind this feminist analysis of parental involvement, I set out to discover whether or not current home–school practices placed pressure on mothers to become more formally involved in their children's education, and if so, whether this pressure had any effect on the mothers and their perception of their mothering role. In other words, is there a relationship between parental involvement and patterns of mothering, and if there is, what is its nature? In addition, the research examined whether the demands of existing practice reinforced or challenged traditional roles of mother as carer, and whether or not this was perceived as problematic by the mothers themselves. It also sought to compare the views of the mothers with those of the headteachers of the schools their children attended.

The research consisted of interviews with 24 mothers of primary 2 (aged six/seven) children from four schools in Glasgow, and parallel interviews with headteachers from each of the same schools. Within each school, six mothers were selected, three of whom were considered to be 'actively involved' and three 'non-involved', with at least one from each category in paid employment. The interviews were structured around the following themes:

- women as mothers;
- mothers and schools;
- perceptions of parental involvement;
- mothers, employment and involvement;
- headteachers and mothers;

and were organised in a way to allow the women the opportunity to talk about and reflect upon their experiences in each of the areas.

A general observation worth noting was that all of the 'involved' mothers and all but two of the 'non-involved' recognised the benefits and gains of parental involvement, regardless of their own levels of participation, and all of the four headteachers were very positive about the gains for both the child and the school.

Women as mothers

In reflecting on the theory and reality of mothering, all of the women expressed a strong conviction that the needs of the child should have primacy over the needs of the mother in the early years (i.e. well into primary school), and three-quarters believed that mothers should be at home full time or part time when their children are young. All agreed that mother as teacher was an integral part of being a good mother, although their interpretation of the teaching role varied considerably from the more formal support for school learning, to the everyday guidance in learning about life. Of particular interest was the fact that ten out of the twelve involved parents saw parental involvement as part of their maternal responsibility, yet only two of the non-involved did despite their equally clear recognition of themselves as teachers. The strongest message that emerged in relation to themselves as mothers, however, was of concerned, caring women who, in the face of enormous demands and pressures, were not only striving to support their children well, but were also doing so, regardless of levels of involvement with the school. Yet only one headteacher gave any recognition at all of the extraordinary pressures of ordinary motherhood that these women were coping with on a daily basis and that were the prime structuring forces in their lives.

Mothers and parental involvement

One observation from the section relating to parental involvement practices in the schools was the marked difference in knowledge of provision available between the involved and non-involved groups of mothers. It would appear that those who are able, or choose, to participate in one or more activities have a greater knowledge of the full range of provision than those who do not. While this could be consequent on a range of factors including access to posters, conversations with teachers, the parental grapevine or individual interest, the fact that the non-involved group showed such a reduced awareness of options available should be of concern to those devising and publicising parental involvement programmes.

Although only one mother in the whole group expressed open dissatisfaction with the school's efforts to involve parents, the majority were either quite or very satisfied, with existing arrangements. Nevertheless it is relevant to mention some of the suggestions offered for improvement because, in the main, they focused upon those areas that the mothers felt were of most importance. They included knowledge of what and how their child was learning, developing improved relationships through informal contact, and a greater openness and honesty between parties. Most also agreed that the best time for them to make these informal contacts was at the beginning or the end of the school day. The implications of this for mothers and teachers are several. From the teacher's perspective, the logistical problems of extending this contact evenly to all parents are enormous, yet if this is perceived to be of prime importance, as it was to the mothers in the study, should it not be an area open for discussion by parents and teachers together?

From the perspective of the mothers, it raises several issues. Firstly, it rewards those who deliver and collect, when the reality is that many mothers use older siblings, other mothers, childminders, or school transport for purely pragmatic reasons. Secondly, it discriminates against the employed mother who is not available at these times, and who is therefore less able, or unable, to make these contacts, and the responses of these mothers give testimony to their feelings of disappointment and guilt at not being there, for the good mother is always available to meet the needs of her child.

The increase in openness and honesty sought by many of the mothers raises questions relating to the power and control of the professional in filtering what is perceived to be appropriate information to the mothers. Significantly, the headteachers saw themselves and their staff as open and truthful, but this perception was not shared by a significant number of mothers. These mothers saw themselves as the recipients of the partial truth in accordance with what the professionals believed they should know, which was not necessarily the same as what the mothers wanted to know.

All the involved mothers recognised the many gains for themselves and their children that resulted from their active involvement with the schools, and these gains demonstrated the undoubted success of the work for those mothers who participated. One disturbing feature, however, suggested by both involved and non-involved mothers, was their perception of increased teacher attention and privilege bestowed upon the children of the 'interested' i.e. involved mothers. However real or imaginary this privilege, the fact that it was suggested by a number of mothers is indicative of some of the pressure that mothers are under to demonstrate their 'interest' in ways that the schools deemed to be appropriate.

While the range of benefits recognised by the involved group demonstrated the positive aspects of parental involvement, they also raised a series of issues relating to the effect of this involvement on mothers. The evidence of the findings suggested that for many, involvement grew as a result of both being in the school, and the more mothers were involved, the more benefits accrued. The consequences of this for the non-involved, and in particular the employed mother, were significant, for not only did it increase the divide between the two sets of mothers, it actively discriminated against the non-involved and her child, and this was clearly articulated by many of the women. It created inequality in a system theoretically geared towards equality, where the criterion for gain was the involvement of the mother. Equally clearly, it sent out strong, if unintentional messages concerning good or appropriate practice for the concerned mother, which rewarded and validated the traditional mothering role. In so doing it served to reinforce one facet of gender inequality, in psychologically impinging upon women's perception of their right to step out of the mothering role and operate, with validity and without censure as 'other than mother'.

When this is considered alongside the findings indicating that 16 of the 24 mothers experienced some pressure to become involved in the school, it presents a strong model of the role the caring mothers should play, and specific reinforcing rewards for those who can and do play it, regardless of the attendant difficulties that they experienced in so doing.

These few examples from the findings of the study indicate some of the ways in which parental involvement operates to regulate mothers, by rewarding the involved and penalising the non-involved, in particular those women who were also in employment. For a third of the mothers agreed that the demands of supporting their children's education made mothering more difficult, and the majority of these were working, or single parents, or both.

Even those who felt that mothering was not necessarily any more *difficult*, added that the demands of schooling did make it *different* from mothering in the past. Maternal participation in education has changed motherhood, and that change, although accepted by many as an automatic part of mothering today, has been policy led rather than parent led.

Headteachers and parental involvement

The headteachers interviewed for the study were caring, concerned professionals who had invested much effort into opening their schools up to parents. All four offered a broad range of parental contacts and programmes, and the mothers were on the whole satisfied with the provision, but there were nevertheless, several problematic issues that emerged during the interviews.

None of the headteachers, all four of whom were women, had any awareness of the gender implications of their parental involvement policy or practice, or the impact that this might have on women as mothers. Neither did any have any sense of the potential inequalities that could, and did, result from their practices. Their personal experiences as women appeared to have little impact upon their professional relationships with the mothers.

Their responses also showed little understanding of the multitude of ordinary pressures that the mothers described so forcefully, or that they could, however inadvertently, be adding to them through either the messages of their parental programmes or through the many requests for assistance that they sent out. In one school in particular, and within the other three to a lesser extent, the responses of the headteachers suggested only a partial understanding of the mothers' agendas, priorities and feelings, for many mothers spoke of barriers, of apprehensions and of lack of honesty in the relationships that were not acknowledged by the headteachers.

The four schools involved offered in total 51 parental activities or programmes, but in all of these, only eight were geared to meet the needs of employed mothers, despite the fact that three of the headteachers recognised that employment patterns militated against involvement. Good mothers are always there, and the timing of the majority of provision rewards those for whom this is true, and excludes those for whom it is not, and the power to determine both the timing and the rewards, lies with the headteacher. Furthermore, all felt that they had not just the power, but the responsibility to intervene in mothering practices if they saw fit, regardless of the fact that none of them was a mother. They understood that teaching parents about their educational role was a part of their professionalism, but when this is considered alongside their limited understanding of the demands and pressures on mothers, it raises serious questions concerning the hidden agenda underpinning much parental involvement in education.

Towards a pro-feminist approach

The main conclusions to emerge from this study highlight above all the need for both parties entrusted with the educational welfare of the child to listen actively to each other, and to hear what each is saying without allocating blame or pressure. For the general picture painted by the respondents was of 24 mothers, each in their own and very different ways, striving to provide the best possible upbringing for their children and, despite the difficulties, recognising that they were, in fact, 'good enough' mothers.

Similarly it portrayed four headteachers, each in their own way, trying to produce what they understood to be the optimum learning environment for the child, which included a recognition of the parental dimension in education. But somewhere in the middle, despite the shared ultimate aim, despite the many areas of agreement, there remained sites of tension and areas of contention in which the mothers were less powerful to voice their agenda and control the outcome.

More significantly, the research confirmed the hypothesis that current forms of parental involvement locate women primarily in their mothering role and thereby reinforce existing gender inequalities, however unintentional this may be.

The majority of the mothers interviewed held conventional views of the mothering role, and the value base underpinning the schools' parental involvement stemmed from a similar ideological paradigm, so the two meshed cosily together in a mutually reinforcing symbiosis where the benefits were significant. The school gained, and the evidence of the headteachers gave testimony to it. The mothers gained a sense of satisfaction and the knowledge that they were being good mothers. In addition, and central to the whole exercise, the child gained, and what stronger spur or motivation could there be for a mother than that which helps and advantages her child?

So it would seem to be a mutually advantageous arrangement until other factors are also considered. They are that:

- this arrangement is premised on one particular limited view of a mother's role that makes clear assumptions about her availability, her lifestyle and her priorities;
- it is centred primarily upon the needs of the school. It is to the school's agenda that the mothers must respond and the agendas of home and school do not always coincide;
- it disadvantages those mothers who cannot or do not conform to this model sending negative messages about themselves as mothers.

This raises a series of difficult issues and questions related to the function of schools, and the role of the professional, particularly given the current proliferation of demands upon teachers. It requires a major re-evaluation of parental involvement which includes a reassessment of its underpinning values, particularly in relation to issues of gender equality. This in turn requires a re-evaluation of professional attitudes and assumptions, and demands that they enter, gender aware, into this crucial, but difficult, area of work.

Parental partnership in education is important, but partnership, not merely involvement, requires a sensitivity to the needs and agendas of both parties concerned, and a recognition that these agendas are not always the same. Above all, if this partnership is to be an empowering one, particularly for mothers, it must recognise that good or 'good enough' mothers are women too in their own right, and incorporate this recognition into the foundations of all practice. Anything less, I believe, does a fundamental injustice to all women, and subverts the true essence of real partnerships in education.

References

Arnot, M. (1993) 'A Crisis in Patriarchy? British feminist educational politics and the state regulation of gender', in Arnot, M. and Weiler, K. (eds) *Feminism and Social Justice in Education*. London: Falmer Press.

Bastiani, J. (1987) *Parents and Teachers 1. Perspectives on home–school relations*. Windsor: NFER-Nelson.

Bastiani, J.(1988) *Parents and Teachers 2. From policy to practice*. Windsor: NFER-Nelson.

Bastiani, J. (1993) 'Parents as Partners: genuine progress or empty rhetoric?', in Munn, P. (ed.) *Parents and Schools*. London: Routledge.

David, M. (1993) *Parents, Gender and Educational Reform*. Oxford: Polity Press.

David, M., Edwards, R., Hughes, M. and Ribbens, J. (eds) (1993) *Mothers and Education: Inside Out?* Hampshire: Macmillan.

Eisenstadt, N. (1988) 'Parental Involvement: some feminist issues', in Browne, N. and France, P. *Untying the Apron Strings*. Milton Keynes: Open University Press.

38

Grant, D. (1989) *Learning Relations*. London: Routledge.

Hall, S., Kay, I. and Struthers, S. (1992) *The Experience of Partnership in Education*. Norfolk: Peter Francis.

Hughes, M., Wikeley, F. and Nash, T. (1994) *Parents and their Children's Schools*. Oxford: Blackwell.

Lareau, A. (1989) *Home Advantage, Social Class and Parental Intervention in Elementary Education*. London: Falmer Press.

Macbeth, A. (1989) *Involving Parents*. London: Heinemann.

Maclachlan, K. (1994) *Parental Involvement in Education and Images of Mothering*, M Ed thesis (unpublished), University of Glasgow.

Merttens, R. et al (eds) (1993) *Ruling the Margins*. London: University of North London Press.

Munn, P. (ed.) (1993) *Parents and Schools*. London: Routledge.

Phoenix, A., Woollett, A. and Lloyd, E. (eds) (1991) *Motherhood: meanings, practices and ideologies*. London: Sage.

Richardson, D. and Robinson, V. (1993) *Introducing Women's Studies*. Basingstoke: Macmillan.

Scott, G. (1989) *Families and Under Fives in Strathclyde*. Glasgow: Strathclyde Regional Council.

Scott, G. (1990) 'Parents and Pre-School Services: issues of parental involvement', *International Journal of Sociology and Social Policy*, 10 (1): 1–13.

Toomey, D. (1989) 'Linking Class and Gender Inequality: the family and schooling', *British Journal of the Sociology of Education*, 10 (4): 389–403.

Walkerdine, V. and Lucey, H. (1989) *Democracy in the Kitchen*. London: Virago.

Weiner, G. (1994) *Feminisms in Education*. Buckingham: Open University Press.

Widlake, P. (1986) *Reducing Educational Disadvantage*. Milton Keynes: Open University Press.

Wolfendale, S. (ed.) (1989) *Parental Involvement: developing networks between school, home and community*. London: Cassell.

Wolfendale, S. (1992) *Empowering Parents and Teachers*. London: Cassell.

4 'It hurts me in my heart when my child brings home a book' – reading at home for bilingual families

Diana Stoker

The words in this title express the feeling of inadequacy and frustration articulated by Syeda Begum. For Syeda, reading with her son poses real difficulties and she dreads it when he brings home a book.

Syeda came to the London Borough of Tower Hamlets twelve years ago. She is a quiet, intelligent woman who lived in Bangladesh until she was sixteen. She attended school in the Sylhet region in the north of the country until she was ten years old and therefore has a basic grasp of literacy in Bengali.

Like so many other women from Bangladesh, she is finding it a slow process to learn English. She goes to classes twice a week but has few opportunities to speak English to anyone except her English tutor and, on occasions, to her child's teacher. She says that although she speaks three languages and can read the Koran in Arabic she can't always understand what the teacher is saying to her about her child and so she just keeps saying, 'Yes, yes', hoping that that is the right answer. She desperately wants her son to succeed at school and would dearly love to help him. How can she support her child? How can the school support her?

Syeda's plight is not uncommon. Thousands of parents from many different countries find themselves in the position of not knowing how to support their children's education but have come to this country with an overwhelming faith in our education system and a belief that our schools will provide an 'open sesame' to a better life for their sons and daughters.

Research shows that where children are supported and helped at home with school subjects, these children do better at school (Tizard and Hughes, 1984; Merttens and Stockton, 1994). The vast majority of teachers would agree with these findings and would look to parents to reinforce and extend children's learning with help and encouragement at home. Although many schools would say they welcome parental involvement – particularly with reading – very few have thought through the implications of what they are asking parents to do and fewer still have been prepared to look at these implications and to come up with solutions to the difficulties they create.

Many teachers would admit that it has taken them considerable time to acquire the skills needed to read a story aloud to a group of children and yet we expect parents to be able to do this at home in a foreign language and without help or guidance.

Syeda graphically describes being *told* stories by her grandfather as they sat under the banyan tree in the cool of the evening at her home in Bangladesh but no one ever *read* her a story from a book. She says she wants help to be able to read to her child.

Although teachers would want to encourage parents to *tell* as well as *read* stories to their children, many Bangladeshi parents underestimate the value of an oral tradition and would want to embrace the norms of the British education system that puts such emphasis on the written word. Many newcomers to this country lose confidence in the important qualities of their own cultural heritage under the pressure to conform to the culture of their newly adopted country. Ironically, in Britain we now look back to find and appreciate our own oral traditions that we have lost but we do little to encourage the storytelling skills of the parents and grandparents who have come from places like Bangladesh or to make the effort to learn from them.

Syeda knows, however, that reading is one of the keys to success for her child but more often than not, she cannot read the books her child brings home. The books are full of words she doesn't know and can't pronounce and even a seemingly simple book like *Mr Gumpy's Outing* has words such as 'the children *squabbled*', 'The chickens *flapped*', 'The sheep *bleated*', and phrases like 'the pig *mucked about*'. She is unlikely to come across words like these in her English class and yet books written for English-speaking children contain idioms and vocabulary that are beyond the experience of the adult learner struggling to acquire the language.

At her own admission, Syeda says she stumbles over the words and finds it hard to read with expression. Her child gets bored and doesn't want to listen. Because her husband speaks better English, she constantly refers her son to his father for help and the child now feels that his mother is inadequate and unable to support him with his school work. She, in turn, has lost her confidence and, worse still, feels she has lost face in the eyes of her child.

Bangladeshi children born in this country have no alternative but to live divided lives between two cultures and, although they will inevitably grow up to reject many of their parents' traditions, it is vitally important that they see their parents as positive role models who have skills, talents and experience to offer their children. It is only with positive role models that these second generation children will be able to find a balanced, secure and fulfilled place in British society. As teachers, we need to put ourselves in the parents' position and imagine the support and help *we* would need if we found ourselves in Bangladesh and were faced with helping our own children learn the language of Nazrule and Rabindranath Tagore.

Some schools would subscribe to the view that parents can *share* books in ways other than reading aloud with their children, but for many parents, both bilingual and native speaking, this 'sharing' concept so casually talked about by teachers is shrouded in mystery and incomprehension for parents.

Teachers say that one way of sharing a book with a child is to look at the pictures, but extending the child's learning and posing open-ended questions that will encourage a meaningful dialogue is all part and parcel of the trained teachers' skills and not all parents feel able to do this effectively without help.

At a recent conference in Strathclyde, a group of English-speaking professionals involved in parent education were asked to take part in an experiment. With a partner, they role played being a parent and child sharing a book at home. The book, however, was written in Bengali and those taking part admitted they found the task difficult to do. The consensus of opinion was that, if you can't understand the text, you become bored and frustrated very easily and that the effort required to make up your own story or to try to make sense of a series of seemingly unrelated pictures takes a great deal of energy and imagination. When the text was explained to them, they were able to share the story more enthusiastically but when asked to repeat one line in Bengali, they were unable to do so.This somewhat superficial experiment did, however, bring home to the professionals the difficulties faced by many parents struggling to 'share' books with their children.

An unexpected opinion voiced by some Bengali parents about children's books in this country concerns the content and quality of the narrative. They explained that all the stories they had been told as children were traditional and, like *Aesop's Fables,* had a strong moral ending. For them, the purpose of a story was to teach the difference between good and evil and to show what happens if one strays from the straight and narrow path. They found many stories in this country pointless because they felt they were not teaching the children anything of value. They said that stories using rhyme were hard to follow and that they couldn't always understand the humour and play on words in certain books.

When asked to choose one book from a huge variety of colourful and well-presented children's books, they all chose from selections of traditional tales. However, on closer examination of some of the most popular modern children's stories such as *Not Now Bernard,* with its message that parents don't always listen to children and *Mr Gumpy's Car,* that shows how if everyone works together they will succeed, the Bengali parents began to realise that there was a subtler message underpinning many modern tales after all. Schools should perhaps be aware that parents find many of our books difficult to relate to and that the selection we offer should include the more familiar stories that are universal. The story of *The Boy Who Cried Wolf* is known in the Asian sub-continent as *The Boy Who Cried Tiger* and the mouse who removed the thorn from the lion's paw exists in some form or other in every culture. Adapting existing books so that an outing 'in a car' becomes an outing 'in a rickshaw' or having a hungry caterpillar eat 'a samosa' instead of 'a sausage' both amuses and involves parents and can lead to parents and children writing stories together that stem from their own experiences.

Parents are often confused about what is expected of them by the school. When a child brings home a book, are they supposed to read it to the child? As already explained, many find this hard to do. Is the child meant to read to the parent? Very often, children bring home books that they have chosen themselves and which are too difficult for them to read unaided. If neither the parent nor the child can read the book with confidence, it is unlikely that either party will consider the book with any degree of enthusiasm and although the children may have chosen a book because they heard it read in school or because they are interested in the subject matter, it may be difficult to convey this interest to their parents when they take the book home.

Supposing that the parents can read the book, how much should they help and correct the child? The teachers themselves have contradictory views on how this should be done and battles rage over the professional correctness of one method over another. Happily, in recent years there has been a move towards the view that 'if it works, don't fix it' and so long as the parent and child are enjoying reading together and progress is being made, then the methods used may not matter. Schools still have a long way to go to demystify the teaching of reading for parents and to admitting that despite all the research, there is no one perfect method and each child has their own unique literacy experiences and understanding that help them become readers (CLPE, 1991a).

It is little wonder that parents often feel happier with reading schemes that repeat words over and over again and show a clear progression from one level to the next. If we want to convince parents that it is important that children are able to enjoy and understand what they read and not just read in parrot fashion, then it is vital that we find ways, through negotiation and consultation, that will be both possible and relevant for all concerned. So often in the past, we have demanded and imposed on parents the ways in which we want them to help their children and have sometimes been disappointed and disillusioned with the results. In recent years, the profession has come to understand that learning to read is a social activity and that children pick up an understanding of the written word not only from books, but also from the world around them. Teachers have begun to value the contributions of the home and wider society in helping children's literacy but often parents are unaware or unconvinced that their contribution is of value.

Talking about pictures in a book, listening to a child retelling a programme seen on TV, reading street and shops signs, buying a comic or reading aloud a letter sent from a relative in their home language are all things that parents do and which help a child become literate. For many parents, however, these activities would seem too informal to be important. The Primary Learning Record developed by the Centre For Language in Primary Education in London has gone a long way to value this kind of support that parents give their children and in the 'parent conferences' that they have developed, teachers encourage parents to talk about the language that takes place at home and to emphasise its importance (CLPE, 1991b).

Having looked at some of the difficulties facing parents, we need to look for further strategies that might help to make the task easier but, at the same time, take into consideration the fact that schools have tended to become more inward-looking to the classroom as a result of the demands placed on them by the National Curriculum.

Firstly, it would help parents like Syeda if schools made working with parents part of the whole-school development plan and consider ways in every area of the curriculum in which the staff, parents and children can work together. These need to be realistic and parents need to be involved at the planning stages and not faced with a *fait accompli* after the staff have already made many of the decisions.

Schools often produce leaflets aimed at helping parents with reading at home. These are nearly always written by the teachers and often use educational jargon. Two experiments in the London Borough of Southwark involved groups of parents in producing booklets that they thought would be helpful to other parents in their school. These groups were facilitated by adult education tutors. Some of the teachers were reticent about the idea at first but were relieved to discover that, in fact, the parents shared most of their own views about reading. The end product of a booklet written *by* parents *for* parents made an enormous impact on both schools. The parents attending the groups found that they learned so much from the process of writing the text and selecting the pictures and the teachers found that their role as consultants rather than initiators gave them new insight into the skills and talents of the parents (Stoker *et al.*, 1991).

Where schools have an open policy for parents to attend storytime at the end of the school day, this has proved very successful. Parents have been able to watch the interaction between the teacher and pupils and, in many cases, this has led to parents feeling confident enough to volunteer to tell and to read stories themselves, both in English and in their home language.

At Sir John Cass's Foundation School in the City of London, parents and teachers have chosen 25 favourite books at nursery and infant level. These have been taped in several languages by a variety of people, including grandparents and older children. Each story is backed up with props, puppets or a game made by parents and staff so that when the child takes home the book, the tape and an activity, there is a range of ways and levels at which the parent and child can work together. The workshops held to make the activities and to tape the stories involved the staff and the parents working side by side and the exchange of ideas during these sessions was positive and enjoyable for everyone.

The parents feel much more able to read these 25 books with their children because they themselves have been involved in the production of the materials and have contributed their own ideas. They have seen and heard the teacher read the books to the children in class, they have listened to the tape with their child at home and have played a game about some aspect of the story. The result has been that parents now feel able to tackle less familiar books that the child brings home. Although it is time-consuming to make the original tapes and activities the interaction between the parents and the school staff has been worth the effort and the school now has a library of tapes and games that will last for several years.

This chapter has concentrated on the difficulties that Syeda and many parents like her experience when trying to support their children's learning at home. These difficulties have been expressed by the parents themselves as they try to understand what the school expects of them and how they can do their best for their own children. Syeda has been helped through attending a Parents' Group attached to a school in the East End of London but staffed by adult education tutors. These tutors, who are trained specifically to work with parents, negotiate the curriculum for each group with those who attend. They are often able to act as a bridge between the school staff and the parents and can help explain how children are taught these days in British schools.

The aim of these groups is to build up the parents' confidence in their role as the most important educators in their children's lives and to encourage them to value their own considerable talents and to share them with their sons and daughters.

The parent education tutors also aim to support the teachers in communicating more effectively with parents. It was in order to improve this communication that a group of Bengali parents from Sir John Cass's

Foundation school took part in the 'Parents Talking About Education Conference' held in September 1993 at the University of Greenwich (Sanderson *et al.*, 1994).

Along with parents from Devon, Corby and Liverpool the parents from Bangladesh explained to the professionals who made up the audience at the conference how they felt about sending their children to schools in this country. They said that at first they thought that all their children ever did in an English school was 'play', but that now, as a result of coming to the Parents' Group, they realised how much and how well the children learned through this so-called 'play'. This had helped them with ideas of things to do at home to encourage their children in a whole number of ways.

Since the conference, other parents have gone on to run an INSET training day where they taught the staff how to do several Bengali crafts. Many parents are now doing a nationally accredited course on how to support their children's learning and at Stewart Headlam School in Bethnal Green, parents developed maths boxes full of games and ideas for number activities which has now gone out to all the families of children in the nursery and reception classes.

If schools want to work effectively with parents, then they must try to put across the message that they need and want the help of parents. They need to find clear, relevant, realistic and enjoyable ways in which parents can help and they need to identify, use and value the parents' skills.

It is only in these ways that parents like Syeda will feel pleasure when her child brings home a book and a real sense of achievement when she is able to help him.

References

CLPE (Centre for Language in Primary Education) (1991a) *The Reading Book*. Webber Row, London SE1 8QW.

CLPE (1991b) *The Primary Learning Record*. Webber Row, London SE1 8QW.

Merttens, R. and Stockton, E. (1994) 'The IMPACT Project in Haringey 1993–1994: raising standards in inner city schools', IMPACT Project, University of North London.

Sanderson, Stobart, Stoker, Whalley (1994) 'Parents Talking About Education', report on the conference and developments.

Stoker, D. 'Parents to Parents: helping our children to read', City Lit, Stukeley Street, London WC2B 5LJ.

Stoker, D., Hegarty, M., Jordan, V., Jaffer, S., Meredith, L., Whipps, M., Green, D. and Ooi, P. (1991) 'The Good Time Reading Guide', City Lit, Stukeley Street, London WC2B 5LJ.

Tizard, B. and Hughes, M. (1984) *Young Children Learning, Talking and Thinking at Home and School*. London: Fontana.

5 Empowering pupils through home–school links

Conrad Chapman

Introduction

Through years of experience within the home–school sphere a number of issues have always seemed worthy of further interest and exploration. One such issue that has increasingly interested the author is that of the underdeveloped role of the 'pupil' within the home–school debate. Despite the obvious presence of pupils within the home–school rhetoric they are almost invariably overlooked in practice. Most home–school activity appears to be carried out, either literally or metaphorically speaking, over the heads of pupils, as if they really did not exist.

Various arguments have been advanced to justify this situation, ranging from the fact that they are too immature, have unrefined reasoning processes, limited experience, no financial stake in the school to being generally apathetic with limited physical and mental prowess to compete with adults (Boltery, 1992).

Thankfully, the above scenario is being challenged from a variety of sources, including SEN Code of Practice (DfE, 1994) where consulting and involving the pupil at each stage is considered an integral part of the process. Again, research projects dealing with home–school collaborations (Jones *et al.,* 1994; Bastiani, 1995) and individual institutions are not only realising but are also strongly advocating that pupils of all ages can, and should be allowed to, participate in and play a direct and increasingly important role in home–school activities, especially in matters relating to themselves.

An empowering influence

The inclusion in and the involvement of pupils in both taking and making decisions that may affect their daily lives within school is a powerful notion to compensate for the views expressed above.

The rest of this discussion will present a scenario for including pupils in many ways within home–school links, together with a range of exciting and innovatory practices that include not only sharing information, responsibility, skills and decision-making, but also make all parties (teachers, parents and pupils) accountable to each other by facilitating this. In a cyclical sense, this enabling process can lead to genuine empowering structures for pupils.

Pupil rights

Through the enactment of the 1988 Education Reform Act in England and Wales it was perceived that pupils were entitled to a broad and balanced curriculum. Essentially, this was conceived as a basic human right. Denying pupils the opportunity to learn could therefore be considered an infringement of that fundamental right. Likewise, Article 12 of the UN Convention on the Rights of the Child (1989) states:

> 1. Parties shall assure to the child who is capable of forming his or her own views the right to express those views freely in all matters affecting the child, the views of the child being given due weight in accordance with the age and maturity of the child.
>
> (p. 5)

Again, the present government in *Choice and Diversity* (DfE, 1992) highlighted the virtues of pupils being involved as decision-makers in educational matters.

Non-implementation of such ideals may well be perceived as an infringement on pupils' basic rights to be listened to, involved in and responded to. Within a so-called democratic and responsible society it is not too difficult to assume that pupils should be listened to, involved in and consulted in an appropriate manner, in accordance with their age, phase and stage of development. Likewise, they should have a right of redress. It would not take much, in these times of greater consumer emphasis, to broaden and extend the spirit of the above, including the Children Act (1989) which recognised the right of the child to be consulted in welfare matters concerning themselves and develop an education tangent capable of legitimising the right of the pupil to be included:

• in decisions about their own actions;
• to express their opinions;
• to be involved in institutional decisions.

The above suggestions, if enacted within schools, would certainly enhance and project the pupil into a centralist role in issues pertinent to themselves. This point is alluded to by Bastiani and Doyle when they suggest that the time is now ripe to, 'revive the Taylor Committee recommendations on formal pupil involvement in school affairs, through representation on governing bodies (or consultative links with the governing body) and representative school councils' (1994: 45).

Pupil involvement in school governance

Interesting developments within the area of school government and including pupils are percolating through education. In accordance with age, phase and stage of development it is possible for pupils to take on membership of governing bodies with respective voting and participation rights. Alternatively, pupils may be afforded 'observer' status of such bodies and while not having voting rights may be encouraged to speak and present a point of view. The symbolic function of this representation does a lot to ensure that the pupil is perceived as a genuine partner in general school affairs.

However, there may be a conflict of interest within the empowering legislation passed by this government, for while the 1986 Education Act increased and encouraged parent involvement in school government, Section 15 of the same Act prohibited pupils/students under the age of eighteen years serving on governing bodies. Despite this there are interesting developments within some educational establishments, especially those with sixth forms and in further education colleges, where flexibility appears to be the order of the day and common, rational thought determines pupils having representation on their respective governing bodies.

Further initiatives, whereby pupils are involved in the political process of the school include them being elected to 'School or Pupil Councils'. The idea is that each class may elect up to two pupils/students to represent them in the monthly 'School Council' on issues which matter to them – from keeping animals at school, to uses of the playground to the start and finishing times of the school. In one Oxfordshire school pursuing this route, democratic classroom elections of representatives has replaced teacher selection. Likewise, the tendency for pupils to go for a 'best pal' have been replaced by considerations of 'fitness for the job'. It would seem that vital political lessons are being learnt here for the pupil especially within the realms of appointing the best person for the post.

Taking this process further and wishing to extend pupil involvement further, pupils have been invited to attend meetings concerning various issues and formulation of policy in areas like homework, behaviour and codes of conduct. According to Boltery (1992) this is based on the assumption that pupils are much more likely to obey policies/rules in which they have had some input or have been instrumental in forming. After all it is a central purpose of schools for students and teachers to devise structures and rules by which they can live together as a community.

In a recent visit the author made to a primary school in Birmingham, the above idea had been extended and not only were pupils throughout the school formulating school and classroom rules, but they were also involved in monitoring resultant behaviours. Consequently, a number of junior pupils had been trained as school–class arbitrators and were being used to counsel pupils who had broken the rules or who had suffered at the hands of a perpetrator.

Contextualising the debate

Most people would acknowledge that it would be inappropriate for children of primary school age to have full control over major decisions which affect their educational opportunities. Certainly as has been noted previously in the discussion children should have the right to be involved in such decision-making, but it could be argued (as noted earlier), that their level of experience, knowledge and intellectual maturity would make it inappropriate, in all instances, for them to have the final say. Even though adults do not always use the most apt criteria when making educational decisions in their child(ren)'s interest, it is a truism to suggest that they are more likely than children to put long-term interests and concerns before immediate wants.

The main argument used in favour of parents' rights in their children's education would appear to derive from the notion that parents must be given those rights which allow them to dispense their responsibilities to care for their child.

Thus, in placing responsibility for a child's education in the hands of the parents, Principle 7 of the United Nations Declaration of the Rights of the Child suggests that the guiding principle should be 'the best interests of the child'. Surely the best interest of the child is served progressively in taking them into account as soon as their intellectual development permits. As White has put it 'Parents ... have obligations as educators, not independent rights as progenitors' (1982: 167), it is also important for a child's personal dignity to feel that their perspective is being taken seriously, and this is most likely when their parents include them in decision-making at an appropriate level as soon as able.

Again, when referring to pupil influence and activity in certain aspects of school process and organisation, one is really only recognising the broad principle of involving those at the heart of and central to the home–school partnership debate. Such a partnership as described by Pugh and De'Ath involves – 'A working relationship that is characterised by a shared sense of purpose, mutual respect, and the willingness to negotiate. This implies a sharing of information, responsibility, skills, decision making and accountability' (1989: 68).

Mediating the above key idea through partnership practices, we acknowledge the changing context within which home–school collaborations are taking place and also the centrality of pupils becoming the main focal point in a variety and range of these collaborations.

Other factors facilitating pupil involvement

Over the last two to three decades Britain has been going through an unprecedented amalgamation of demographic changes. Large-scale unemployment on the present scale has not been witnessed since the depression of the 1930s and has left many on state benefits. Of the new employment opportunities, many are temporary, short-term, part-time and are occupied by women. Likewise, the incidence of children being reared in one-parent families has increased, owing to a variety and range of factors (i.e. higher incidence of divorce, greater financial stability on the part of one partner) (Utting, 1995). Again, many inner-city areas have become ethnic minority enclaves where it is not unusual for a variety of reasons (including skills in speaking English as a second language, differing school perceptions/expectations and low self-esteem) for schools to be all but devoid of parental involvement and contact. These and other reasons are advanced as to why parents are not often available for consultation or involvement in their children's education.

Developing practice in such instances

Many schools do not challenge the above scenario and while seeking to offer opportunities for parents to make contact or get involved, are switching their attention to their pupils or attempting to contact older pupils to act as surrogate parents to younger brothers and sisters. The latter are expected to fill or plug the parental void and act in many ways as mediators between home and school, or even substitute parents, shaping both attitudes and behaviour towards home–school links.

It is not uncommon to find older brothers and sisters involved in both 'Shared Reading' and 'Paired Reading' projects with younger siblings. This process acts as a bridge between the stages of reading to children and children reading to themselves. Increasingly, older siblings are encouraged to attend support sessions at school, at mutually convenient times, to illustrate and support the above projects. Again, older siblings are encouraged to record progress and make key statements regarding the reading activity. The above strategies are not new and were popularised by proponents like Topping (1987) who noted gains in reading accuracy and comprehension where the above processes were used. The parent/ older sibling is encouraged to give frequent praise and to respond to errors by simply giving the correct word which the child repeats or allowing the latter to take control of reading process when they feel ready by giving a sign, such as tapping their older sibling's hand. There is no discussion or any attempt to get the child to analyse the word phonically. Also important is the ability of the parent/older sibling to maintain fluency by sliding easily back into simultaneous reading mode. The experience becomes fun for the child who feels in charge of the situation, choosing his or her book and controlling movements to independent reading.

Other curriculum areas have been developed in the same way. IMPACT maths has taken on the same status as shared reading and partnership process between pupils–teachers and older siblings are being positively encouraged and developed. Merttens and Vass (1990) noted a most interesting observation when evaluating early IMPACT projects in schools. They claim:

> That in a substantial number of tasks children were acting as the tutors in the home. It turned out that the children perceived themselves as knowing more about what had to be done than their parents. Even nursery aged children got into the role of initiator and organiser of the activity.
>
> (p. 13)

This 'mediator/substitute' role between home and school is constantly being extended into other spheres of schooling activity. Many older children visit the school on 'parents' days/evenings' and attend 'reporting of progress' sessions. The responsibility that such commitment brings, and also the sincerity of effort that goes into effecting these changes in perception, is required by all partners.

Onward to independence: another factor

Johnson and Ransom (1983) noted that as pupils reached the junior/secondary transition stage and moved into the later phases of their education, some parents took this is an opportunity to review their own behaviour and attitudes towards their child(ren)'s education. Many parents, the former concluded, viewed this as a time to make a break, or to step up the phased withdrawal which had slowly been taking place since earlier school years. The perspective appeared to be forward to employment and independence rather than backwards to pre-school years dependency. Accompanied and accelerated by parental perceptions of bigger establishments, more teachers, more formalised set meetings (usually of the open evening and prize evening variety), has left schools rethinking their partnership processes/practices and attempting to focus more on the rich vein of interest of the pupil.

In some instances the way forward has been in projecting the role of the pupil, as stated previously, into a more centralist position acting as a catalyst for further activity. A developing practical example includes the involvement of pupils in three-way discussions about progress. At North Area College, Stockport, the student is encouraged to set annual/termly targets that are then reviewed periodically with other partners. Thus, the student takes charge of the process and is central to curriculum and procedural issues concerning themselves. It is the students who activate the mechanism to involve others at appropriate times to coincide with their planning and time targets.

Likewise, the crucial importance now attached to pupils contributing to and being involved in their own achievement and development can be perceived in the increasing importance given to techniques such as Records of Achievement (ROA) particularly, but not exclusively, in the secondary school. The author is reminded of the excellent practices evolving from nursery phases – of the child actively being involved in recognising both their academic and personal achievements. Good examples of such practices are noted along lines suggested by Wolfendale (1990) in the development of her booklet *All about Me,* which is used extensively and increasingly, not only with teachers and parents but also with pupils at pre-school and on entry to school phases. Likewise, at Monson Primary School in New Cross, London, they have sought to use the ROA as a tool for developing partnerships among all partners. Nursery children, using loose-leaf folders, are encouraged to add their drawings; photographs of pupil activity are also included in charting the pupil's development. At other phases and stages, especially as the child goes onward and upwards towards independency, ROA increasingly encourage the pupil/student to review recent progress and targets, and develop further personal action plans leading to new targets and development. Once such a procedure has been accomplished then further support and resourcing structures may then be identified and ascribed. Through a celebration of progress and development through the ROA, the pupil is projected more and more into a partnership role. This then facilitates and motivates greater commitment and ownership. The ROA are not unproblematic, however, with the dichotomy of interested partners being perceived in the general discussion concerning who the ROA is for – the teacher, the parent, the child or all. The conclusion of this debate may well influence the range, form, style, structure and organisation of the ROA.

Again, pupils are increasingly being used to explain aspects of their curriculum, either at 'Review' meetings, as above or during workshop sessions for parents to explain various aspects of the curriculum. More and more pupils are being included in the planning stages of the workshops, for both initiation and delivery. They are involved too in not only setting workshop programmes and agendas, but also in making resources and explaining their educational significance to their parents. This idea of children showing and explaining their school work to their parents has really taken off at schools like Rush Common in Abingdon. We note that at reading workshop, 'after ten minutes or so, the children took over the reading session doing their presentations, sharing their book reviews, playing games and looking at boxes of new books' (Jones *et al.*, 1994: 38).

The idea that parents are more motivated by seeing the direct relevance to their own child and, therefore, are more likely to attend can be, and often is, found to be true.

In some instances, the sharing, explaining and interpreting of ideas has been further developed with pupils publishing and editing their own school and class papers and newsletters. This is a developing theme in many schools but is being used to good effect by using the pupil focus to inform and motivate parents.

Listening and responding: the pupil view

In developing genuine partnership process with pupils, an essential characteristic on the part of schools and teachers is the ability to listen to other partners (Atkin *et al.*, 1988), especially the pupils themselves. Pupil Councils, mentioned earlier, can be a means of doing this, but another truly pioneering area of development is the use of a questionnaire to ascertain pupil views and opinions. Macbeath *et al.* (1992), who helped establish and develop the notion, noted rich avenues of exploration through the use of such techniques and also the disparate views among pupils, parents and teachers. Within the realm of homework for instance, obvious differences of opinion between the partners were noted, which from a school planning point of view could and would tend to raise all manner of questions around the notion of communications and the homework policy itself. However, a further point of worth regarding questionnaire development evolves around schools latching on to pupil views and opinions which can then be used in effective development planning, from curricular materials on survey methodology for instance, to gender or personal and social education issues. At Greenhill Community School, in Oldham, where the author works, pupil surveys are conducted throughout the school on a regular basis. A range of opinion is sought on a wide variety of issues, from play and lunch-time facilities through to classroom and homework facilities for pupils. Through these techniques an important message is being mediated to the pupil, and it concerns their right as a consumer of the school product, to be listened to and have, where appropriate, their view considered.

It means a change of views on all fronts

The author is not so naïve to believe that such a change in power structures can be achieved simply or quickly. Many partners, especially teachers will not find it easy to loosen control and begin to listen to significant others, especially when one of those others might be their pupils. While many parents have long realised the centrality of their children in initiating, building and consolidating home–school relations, in many instances, this is not a view shared with quite the same purpose by a number of teacher colleagues. Some of the latter may find it neither relevant nor practical to seek positive partnership practices with their pupils, others might believe it could compromise and destroy the point, for example, of meetings with parents. Such professional views, as expressed above, are becoming more and more eroded and are being usurped by a belief that in any form of home–school relationships, pupils must have a central and unmistakable role to play. Again, this would appear to be a sentiment shared by many parents, who realise that many views surrounding school and the conditions of classroom life are procured through the pupil, both directly and indirectly. In addition, the actual form and content of these relations are formed and effected by the personality of the child(ren), their basic attitudes to school life and work and their success as pupils. Within these circumstances pupils become a crucial influence in the main of home–school relations themselves. The evidence continues to grow, activities projecting pupils to the fore, allowing them to take and make decisions that affect their learning environment are numerous. In the wake of this momentum, professional colleagues owe it to their profession, to their pupils to reach out, be affected by and learn to enter into genuine partnerships with their pupils. Ultimately, if we are all interested in and serious about raising pupil achievements then we owe it to the latter, for all the reasons noted within this discussion, to listen to them and treat them progressively as equals, with an increasingly important role to play in their education.

Conclusion

It is certainly true that merely giving pupils a voice, or allowing them to find one, does not constitute empowerment in enabling them to make and take educational decisions. There are those such as Troyna (Troyna and Carrington, 1990) at Warwick University, who would suggest that genuinely empowering pupils, who are presently at the bottom of the pecking order, is likely to be a long, complicated and at times painful process, which will entail more than simply allowing them the space to express a view. Few would dispute this and in that direction the author has attempted to present a balanced account within this discussion. On the one hand, through an exploration of pupil rights and changing demographic circumstances – the pupil has been projected to the fore. The implication in all this is that denying the latter a voice in the process suggests more about the schools and the society in which they exist than it does about pupils' abilities. On the other hand the empowering activities increasingly being developed throughout some establishments have been noted as good practice in the hope that others planning and developing within this sphere might take heart and not feel that they are working alone in such an essential area of home–school partnership debate.

References

Atkin, J., Bastiani, J. and Goode, J. (1988) *Listening to Parents: an approach to the improvement of home–school relations.* London: Croom Helm.

Bastiani, J. (1995) *Parents in a Learning Society,* Project Study. London: Royal Society of Arts.

Bastiani, J. and Doyle, N. (1994) *Home and School: building a better partnership.* London: National Consumer Council.

Boltery, M. (1992) *The Ethics of Educational Management.* London: Cassell.

Children Act (1989) London: HMSO.

Department for Education (1986) *Education Act.* London: HMSO.

Department for Education (1988) *Education Reform Act.* London: HMSO.

Department for Education (1992) *Choice and Diversity – A New Framework for Schools.* London: HMSO.

Department for Education (1994) *Code of Practice on the Identification and Assessment of Special Educational Needs.* London: HMSO.

Johnson, D. and Ransom, E. (1983) *Family and School.* London: Croom Helm.

Jones, G., Bastiani, J., Chapman, C. and Bell, G. (1994) *A Willing Partnership.* London: Royal Society of Arts.

Macbeath, J., Thomson, B., Arrowsmith, J. and Forbes, D. (1992) *Using Ethos Indicators in Primary School Self Education: taking account of the views of pupils, parents and teachers.* The Scottish Office: Education Department.

Merttens, R. and Vass, J. (1990) *Sharing Maths Cultures: IMPACT – inventing maths for parents and children and teachers.* London: Falmer Press.

Pugh, G. and De'Ath, E. (1989) *Working Towards Partnership in the Early Years.* London: National Children's Bureau.

Topping, K. (1987) 'Paired Reading: a powerful technique for parent use', *The Reading Teacher*, 40: 608–15.

Troyna, B. and Carrington, B. (1990) *Education, Racism and Reform*. London: Routledge.

United Nations Convention (1989) 'Rights of the Child', in Docking, J. (1990) *Primary Schools and Parents: rights, responsibilities and relationships*. London: Hodder and Stoughton.

Utting, D. (1995) *Family and Parenthood: supporting families, preventing breakdown*. York: Joseph Rowntree Foundations.

White, J. (1982) *The Aims of Education Restated*. London: Routledge and Kegan Paul.

Wolfendale, S. (1990) *All About Me*. Nottingham: NES–Arnold.

6 Home–school liaison: the mainstreaming of good ideas and effective practice

John Bastiani

This chapter sets out to explore a home–school issue of growing concern. Improving the quality and effectiveness of its work is now seen as a key task for all schools and all teachers. This task is complemented by the continuing contribution of those with a special responsibility for home–school work, usually through a variety of funded programmes and initiatives.

How can these two bodies of need and experience be brought together more effectively? How can each listen to, learn and benefit from each other? In particular, how can teachers in mainstream schools utilise and develop good ideas and effective practice, in widely differing settings and circumstances.

In recent years there has been a massive increase of interest in relationships between parents and their children's schools. The government, driven by a mixture of ideology and opportunism, has obliged schools to take parents into account in more obvious ways than before; there is now also considerable evidence which confirms the view that positive informed interest and active support actually benefits pupil achievement in tangible and lasting ways.

Finally, there is reason to believe that more and more parents sense an entitlement to be more actively involved in their children's education, both through participation in the life and work of their schools and through membership of a growing number and range of parent organisations and initiatives (Bastiani and Doyle, 1994; Wolfendale, 1992).

This profound shift in the basic relationships between families and schools has occurred, as many of us know only too well, at the same time as an unprecedented period of turmoil and change throughout the educational service as a whole. This includes the introduction of the National Curriculum, new patterns of assessment, devolved budgets, open enrolments, the introduction of a new Code of Practice for children with special educational needs and new arrangements for the formal inspection of schools, to mention but a few!

At the same time, progressive and swingeing cuts in resources and support for vital home–school work is particularly affecting children in city schools. This has happened as a result of shifts in the mainstream budgets and through cuts to the Urban Programme, City Challenge and Section 11 funding (for minority ethnic pupils and their families). Such cuts combine to create a situation where those of us with a commitment to, and active involvement in, home–school work, find there is escalating pressure to:

- continue to make the case for our work and to support this more effectively with information and evidence illustrating what has been achieved;
- find ways in which this work can be more effectively utilised across a wider range of situations and circumstances;
- accommodate new and sometimes paradoxical demands from the government and from parents themselves;
- identify lessons that have been, or need to be, learned and use these to plan further development;
- do all this as part of a growing need to re-assess the appropriateness and continuing relevance of our original intentions, goals and principles, to see whether they still apply.

Against this wider background, there seem to be a number of points of reference, relevant to this chapter. Firstly, among politicians from the different parties, there is, currently, a considerable (I nearly wrote 'depressing'!) amount of consensus. In this consensus (exemplified by the two versions of the Parent's Charter), political interest in parent entitlement focuses upon the provision of information and evidence, relating to both the progress of individual pupils and the life and work of the school as a whole, and the way it is formally accountable. In such a view parents are seen as *consumers,* supported by 'A framework for education which gives parents more choice, more and better information and the right to be heard if they think things are going wrong' (Baroness Blatch, NCPTA Conference, Birmingham, DfE News 102/94).

While a succession of legal requirements have had widely differing effects upon schools and families according to their type, situations and circumstances, one thing is clear. Singly, or together, government legislation or administrative requirements do *not* offer either an adequate or credible version of how things might be, or a satisfactory basis for the planning of a school's work with its parents. Indeed, while politicians of all kinds have their own distinctive agendas these do not seem, at present, to be obviously connected to the everyday concerns of *real* parents, families and other carers.

Secondly, for those who are committed to a wider view of education in general, and home–school work in particular, a certain amount of agonising is taking place. At the heart of this is an important shift of emphasis, rather than substance. For while home–school liaison work continues to embrace the spirit of 'partnership' between families and schools, more recent thinking and development is attempting to:

- be clearer about our principles and more self-critical about both what we achieve and what remains to be done;
- find relationships and ways of working that complement and extend existing practice;
- recognise and utilise more effectively, not only common ground and shared responsibility, but also differences of role, perspective and experience, between school and family life.

In this area, the role of specially funded, creative development projects, though few in number, continue to have a crucial contribution to make in the development of fresh-thinking and innovative practice. Two projects that are doing this (although in *very* different ways) are the 'Parents in a Learning Society' Project, based at the RSA (Bastiani, 1995) and the Ferguslie Park 'Home School Employment Project', funded through the Urban Programme (*see* Chapter 9).

Such initiatives are located against a background in which the main ingredients are:

- a widespread set of explanations (not always held with enthusiasm!), that working effectively with parents, families, and others who have responsibility for the education, welfare and development of children, is a key task for all schools and all teachers. This applies regardless of the age of the pupils or the nature of the school – though important differences here will obviously shape the particular approaches that are likely to be effective.
- a rich body of professional knowledge, confidence and skills, based on substantial and often long-standing experience of home–school work, both additionally funded and supported through mainstream budgets. This is giving rise to a growing sense of parental expectation and entitlement and a corresponding belief that families and schools can, and should, work together.

The main task of this chapter is to begin to explore some of the ways in which these two sets of needs and experience can be brought to bear more productively on one another, especially at the school level. It therefore shares a similar agenda to those other contributions in the collection, which look at these issues from the wider viewpoints of LEAs and funded projects respectively.

Role of LEA programmes and initiatives

There can be no doubt that the power of LEAs has been enormously eroded in the home–school field, as elsewhere, by government ideology and policy over a long period. Its capacity, therefore, to provide a framework for initiative and support has correspondingly suffered and there have been all too many examples of both spectacular closures of well-known schemes and a less obvious and more gradual scaling down of commitment and resources.

A recent compilation of UK initiatives by the present author (Bastiani, 1993), however, provides a positive reminder and clear evidence of both the long-term nature and the role of continuing support for additionally funded home–school liaison work. Authorities such as Coventry and Liverpool, and the former Humberside and Strathclyde have achieved a great deal and offer many lessons to be learned.

Firstly, these programmes have contributed hugely to the development of a repertoire of 'good practice' and a culture of positive achievement in which home–school work makes a big contribution. While there are, of course, considerable variations of both content and emphasis, this would typically include:

- a broad and varied programme of practical links and activities;
- home visiting;
- family learning sessions;
- running parent groups/courses;
- outreach work, both with community groups and a range of other agencies.

In almost all cases, the key strategy in the work at the school level has been the appointment and support of a member of staff (coordinated by the LEA) with a special commitment to, and responsibility for, home–school work, together with a degree of funded support for their release, at least on a part-time basis, to carry out this work, within a neighbourhood setting.

Increasingly, too, partly as a response to the changing world, partly as a function of growing confidence and experience, there has been, in every case, a shift of emphasis. This has served to refocus energy and effort away from the concentration of resources in a relatively small number of 'project schools' towards a responsibility to the LEA's service to schools as a whole.

This has sharpened the need to develop ways of working that are both appropriate to a wider range of settings and circumstances and to create a need to ensure the continuity of this work, which has been largely primary based, into secondary schools, in ways that acknowledge their considerable differences. This is already happening and is a major point of growth in current home–school work (*see* Chapter 13).

Secondly, this shift of emphasis is being achieved by the development of more effective networks for sharing ideas and experience. This is being developed by the production of newsletters, a more effective use of the local press and the percolation of 'good practice' through dissemination strategies. Above all, though, it is being achieved through training, INSET and staff development activities, both within schools and across LEAs, increasingly run by local practitioners from 'project schools' themselves. This gives the work both 'street cred' and a status that has greater influence and more noticeable effects.

Categorically funded programmes and initiatives

Cuts and reductions in dedicated expenditure on home–school liaison work have, rightly, received much attention and criticism in recent years. Such setbacks, however, should not blind us to the continuing presence and impact of home–school work in a range of substantially funded programmes. One of the main difficulties in both recognising this, and assessing its impact and achievements, is that such work with parents and families is itself part – often a hidden part – of a wider agenda.

In this section, a number of the best known programmes are outlined, in terms of their relevance to the main ideas of this chapter.

Section 11 funded home–school liaison schemes – for work with minority ethnic parents and families

In spite of the recent restoration of some of the original government cuts as a result of public counter pressure, home–school liaison continues to have a precarious existence within both its respective Section 11 services and in the life and work of schools. This has much to do with the way in which this work is continuously redefined, by the government, by Section 11 services locally and by teachers themselves, in narrow terms of language development and classroom learning. Such an emphasis denies the clear and unequivocal evidence of the strong central relationships between ethnicity, family background and pupil achievement.

Section 11 services at the LEA level have tended to adopt one of two very different strategies. On the one hand, they designate home–school liaison work as an area of responsibility for *all* their staff; on the other, they establish specialist teams and posts, with HSL responsibility to work alongside language support staff. Either way, their work is marginalised or even ignored, if there is not a clear, widespread understanding of its significance in children's learning, behaviour and achievement. A recent OFSTED survey recognises the importance and contribution of Section 11 funded HSL work (OFSTED, 1994).

HSL work within a multicultural setting has both adapted mainstream practices, such as the more effective use of community languages, and developed its own distinctive approaches and expertise. This mixture of initiative and response is portrayed in Figure 6.1.

> ■ The provision of specialist staff to initiate and support home–school liaison work through home visiting, parent support groups, work with other members of staff etc.
> ■ The recruitment and training of parents to work alongside teachers as bilingual classroom assistants
> ■ The involvement of parents in the life and work of the school
> ■ The use of pupils as key links between the language of the school and that of the home
> ■ Translation and interpretation services (now helped by software); information in community languages
> ■ Liaison with supplementary schools, local mosques etc.
> ■ Responsiveness to parents' own educational needs and development: adult classes etc.
> ■ Provision of independent advocacy, information, advice and support (especially for newly arrived families)
>
> **(Bastiani, 1994)**

Figure 6.1 Some strategies for working with ethnic minority parents and families

Until the recent imposition of the Single Regeneration Budget, the government continued to fund a wide range of educational programmes in which working with parents was a significant feature of a wider agenda. Not surprisingly the resource level for such programmes has been severely reduced and LEA bids have become increasingly competitive and stage managed by the government.

The common focus of such initiatives is the bringing together of a 'package' of strategies which combine to raise pupil achievement, within the aegis of the Urban Programme, especially in Scotland, City Challenge and GEST 19 (then 34), 'Raising Pupil Standards in Inner Cities'. Funded programmes are separately and specifically funded, for up to three years, but reviewed annually. Several examples are featured in this collection. (An interesting exception here is Cleveland's unusual, but aptly named 'Community Coalition Project', which brings a number of these separate strands together in a planned, coherent way.)

The 'pupil achievement' agenda

This typically includes strategies to develop:

- 'school improvement';
- pupil behaviour (including truancy/attendance linked funded initiatives);
- basic skills work (especially in reading development and maths including, briefly, the Reading Recovery linked work);
- involving parents – through better understanding of and support for, their children's school learning (e.g. IMPACT Maths).

Here, as in Section 11 work, there is enormous variation in the extent to which the home–school work is an integral part of the approach as a whole, or a rather token part of it. Unlike Section 11 work, however, the work with parents tends to be handled as a whole-school task, rather than a specialist responsibility.

Two more recent developments are worthy of mention here. Firstly, the Family Literacy Programme, funded by the DfE through the Basic Skills Agency, tackles, as the name makes clear, an area of widespread concern within home–school work. Interesting features, both of its Demonstration Projects and Small Grants Programme are the obligation for schools and adult basic education provision to work productively together. This reinforces the view, rather played down in recent years, that pupil achievement and parents' own education and development are, in reality, inextricably bound up with one another. The other interesting feature of this programme is the contribution it makes to the concept of family learning, in which adults and children learn together. While this has been a marked feature of Scottish home–school work, it has been rather undervalued 'south of the border'.

Finally, home–school work promises to make a greater and more significant contribution to work with children with special educational needs and their families, in the wake of the new Code of Practice. There does seem to be a genuine and significant shift of ideology and official attitude, made explicit in both the Code itself and in the Guide for Parents (DfE, 1994a). Here parents are stated to have a genuine partnership role with schools, based on parents' own, unique knowledge of their own child, acknowledged for the first time.

> Children's progress will be diminished if their parents are not seen as partners in the educational process with unique knowledge and information to impart. Professional help can seldom be wholly effective unless it builds upon parents' capacity to be involved and unless parents consider that professionals take account of what they say and treat their views and anxieties as intrinsically important.
>
> (DfE, 1994b: 13)

That this shift of rhetoric is genuine can also be seen, to some extent, in the proposed new structures and processes for the statementing of special needs and in the allocation of relatively encouraging Grants for Education Support and Training (GEST) funding to support related training and professional development. This includes funding for the appointment of LEA Partnership Officers, to work more productively with parents, and for school-based INSET. As has happened before, the world of SEN has raised issues in a particularly heightened way, that has impact for both the thinking and practice of schools generally.

In this section, an attempt has been made to summarise a number of the major, funded home–school programmes and activity currently existing in Britain. At the same time I have suggested a number of widespread, shared concerns and developments, that cut across the considerable differences between the different situations. Above all, it is now a good time to acknowledge, and make accessible, some of the *key lessons* that can be learned from this body of experience in terms of their potential impact upon the life and work of each school as a whole. The rest of this chapter looks at some of the ways in which this work can be utilised and given legitimacy, for teachers and schools of all kinds across the education service.

'Mainstreaming' and 'embedding' good practice

In recent years references to 'mainstream' situations and to 'embedding' as a process have become widespread and have achieved significant currency and extensive usage. Closer analysis, however, reveals that there is more to it than meets the eye! Since this account wishes to draw upon a range of meanings that have accrued, it is necessary to summarise some of the possibilities.

Mainstream in terms of this chapter refers to schools, teachers and classrooms which are part of the education service as a whole, funded from the mainstream budgets. Special projects and programmes are separately or additionally funded with teachers on individual different contracts, which can often heighten their sense of vulnerability.

Mainstream schools and classrooms can also be used to differentiate those (the majority) which do *not* contain minority ethnic, bilingual, statemented or other pupils with special educational needs. In this sense, mainstream is used as a broad term to distinguish between things that are general and typical of wider populations and circumstances and those that are the product of special needs provision and treatments.

Similarly embedding describes processes whose function is to encourage and support adaptation and assimilation, so that activities that were previously distinctive, special or separate, can enter and become part of the normal, regular way of going about things – for everyone.

In home–school terms, mainstreaming can be seen to cover a range of these possibilities. It can suggest:

- bringing a school's work with parents and families closer to the life and work of the school as a whole. This has, of course, considerable implications for the way in which a school collectively plans, organises and evaluates its home–school work. It also tends to raise the profile of such work, confers greater legitimacy upon it, raises its status and, as a result, its impact.
- a common set of legal requirements and contractual obligations that apply universally, without significant differentiation, across the system. These include parental rights to express a preference of school, information for parents, evidence of pupil achievement and the representation of parents in the government of schools.
- making work with parents a key task for all schools and all teachers, rather than the responsibility of paid specialists, or committed and enthusiastic 'volunteers'. A key strategy here is the development of a 'whole-school' approach.

This is given further weight by the significance currently attached to:

- *whole-school themes and processes,* such as reading and language development, recording, reporting and assessment, pastoral care, etc.;
- *policy-linked practice,* which has recently spread to pupil behaviour/anti-bullying, homework and home-learning and equal opportunities.

- incorporating the knowledge, skill and experience of people with a specialist involvement in relevant areas. This applies especially to general home–school liaison work, to work with minority ethnic pupils and families, and to statemented pupils with a range of special educational needs and their families. This may require both the more effective use of special experience *and* its adaptation for wider use. Currently, for example, the survival of much Section 11 funded HSL work is dependent upon the ability of schools to learn how this can be done, through, for example, the more effective utilisation of home visits.
- the adoption and/or adaptation of new ideas and practices, project and programme initiatives, etc. in ways that enable them to become part of the school's 'normal' way of going about its work. A very special feature of such possibilities is the increasing wish of parents to be consulted and to contribute to the life and work of their children's schools in a variety of ways. This is matched, to some extent, by the

perception of an increasing number of teachers and schools that this is not only necessary, but helpful to the school's development and to pupil achievement. There is, of course, a wide range of match and mismatch here!

■ finally, and logically, the extent to which effective home–school work is genuine and embedded in the life and work of schools as a whole is rapidly becoming one of the criteria by which the quality of a school's work is judged – by teachers, in their review of their efforts and achievements – by OFSTED inspectors, and by parents themselves, both through the initial choice of their children's school and in their continuing confidence and trust in what it is doing.

Developing home–school work: Catch 22 re-visited

Figure 6.2 Catch 22

- To develop effectively, work with parents, families and other carers needs to become an integral part of the life and work of all schools and all teachers.
- When the idea and practice of working effectively with parents is accepted as a basic requirement and a professional obligation for all teachers, it changes in character and form.

A focus on home–school philosophy and practice in mainstream schools and staff rooms, brings a number of shadowy issues crisply into focus. Typically, these concern the nature and demands that are currently being made upon schools and teachers and the extent to which:

- positive attitudes and genuine support for their work exists and can be built upon;
- there are available sources of knowledge, skill and experience that can be tapped;
- other resources, of funded time, energy and practical materials exist;
- there are perceived and actual benefits and satisfactions from work in this area;
- ideas for existing initiatives and proposed developments are seen to be practicable.

My impression, for what it's worth, is that, at the time of writing, many schools are somewhere in the middle of this dilemma. Firstly, there is widespread acceptance, in schools of all kinds, of both the case for and benefits of, developing practical forms of cooperation. However, few schools seem yet to have developed effective mechanisms and ways of working that enable this to grow and be consolidated on a school-wide basis. So existing work remains patchy, uneven and sometimes, as far as parents are concerned, infuriatingly inconsistent.

Secondly, while beginning to recognise some of the achievements and potential contributions of specialist home–school liaison roles and expertise, we are not yet able to tap into it as well as we might. This is particularly true where the work is visible or requires obvious skill and experience, such as home visiting in school hours, running adult groups, bilingual work, etc.

We're still inclined to marginalise this work and limit its contribution by saying, of colleagues with special responsibility, 'It's their job: they're paid to do it!' Such work is still too often considered as a separate strand, rather than a contribution to the school's core development through the collection of parent views, planning of INSET, running discussions and establishing links with community groups and organisations.

In fact, we need *both* elements – the general development of the capacity of all members of staff to develop together within a policy-led, whole-school approach (e.g. Alexander *et al.*, 1995) *and* the special contributions of those who have designated responsibilities, or a particular contribution to make through a combination of personality, commitment and experience. And we need these two elements to work *together* and to be mutually responsive.

There is likely to be, in most schools, a broad agenda of activity and concern, in which there is considerable scope for them to focus their current efforts, to see what lessons can be learned from previous experience and elsewhere, and where development is both desirable and possible! Recent examples include the identification of home–school work as a priority in school development plans or as a follow-up to OFSTED inspection. Such an agenda, which would, incidentally, be suited to a list that many parents would also draw up, has considerable scope to transform the character and effectiveness of a school's work with parents. Figure 6.3 gives a few examples to be getting on with.

Finally, to maintain a culture of professional learning and development in which this kind of growth is encouraged and supported, we still need both LEA and national development projects (of the kind described in other contributions in this collection). For here it is still possible to find the space and provide the focus for trying out new ideas and practice, and to take some of the moderate risks in our thinking and experience that make accelerated learning possible.

Figure 6.3 Examples for a broad agenda of activity and concern

Arrangements for new parents
(Information: meetings: home visits) Issues of transfer and continuity

Recording, reporting, assessment
(Written reports: teacher/parent/pupil)

Parents as co-educators
- Homework and home learning
- How parents can help their children's (school) learning
- Family learning etc.

Keeping parents informed: giving them a voice
Enlisting their support for the life and work of the school.
(Parent governors: parent newsletters: parent organisations etc.)

Involving parents in policy and decision-making in key areas
e.g. curriculum links (sex/religious education) homework, anti-bullying pupil behaviour, anti-racism/equal opportunities/special needs

Developing a whole-school, home–school approach that includes:
- Regular review of current efforts
- Incorporation of parental views and expectations
- Producing a negotiated written policy
- INSET, training and professional development

References

Alexander, T., Bastiani, J. and Beresford, E. (1995) *Home–School Policies: a practical guide.* JET Publications, 67 Musters Rd, Ruddington, Nottingham NG11 6JB.

Bastiani, J. (1993) *UK Directory of Home–School Initiatives.* London: RSA.

Bastiani, J. (1994) Extracts taken from a 'Briefing Paper' for the 'Intercultural Education Project' Conference at Stratford upon Avon. Contact author.

Bastiani, J. (1995) *Taking a Few Risks: learning from each other; teachers, parents and pupils.* London: RSA.

Bastiani, J. and Doyle, N. (1994) *Home and School: building a better partnership.* London: National Consumer Council.

Department for Education (1994a) *Special Educational Needs – a guide for parents.* London: Department for Education.

Department for Education (1994b) *Code of Practice on the Identification and Assessment of Special Educational Needs.* London: Department for Education.

OFSTED (1994) *Educational Support for Minority Ethnic Communities.* A report from OFSTED, reference 130/94/NS. OFSTED, Publications Centre, PO Box 151, London E15 2HN.

Wolfendale, S. (1992) *Empowering Parents and Teachers: working for children.* London: Cassell.

7 The PSP experience in Liverpool: towards a city-wide service

The Liverpool Parent School Partnership

Background

The Liverpool Parent School Partnership (PSP) was established in 1979 with funds from central government's Inner City Partnership Initiative. The White Paper, *Policy of the Inner Cities,* published in June 1977, emphasised the commitment to regenerating inner city areas by means of:

- strengthening their economies and thereby the prospects of those who live in them;
- improving their physical fabric and making the environment more attractive;
- alleviating social problems;
- securing a new balance between the inner areas and the rest of the city region, in terms of population and jobs.

In Liverpool the government, the Area Health Authority, Liverpool City Council and the then Merseyside County Council entered into arrangements to prepare programmes of action to tackle these problems over the next decade. Included in the education programme was the innovatory concept of the Parent Support Programme to be based at a number of primary schools in the inner area of the city. It was considered that social environment and particularly levels of parental interest and support were major elements in the determination of pupil attainment.

The 'project', originally named the Parent Support Programme, was based initially in seventeen inner city schools where parent centres were established, in the most part using space that had been released through falling rolls. These newly equipped centres were staffed by two extra workers (an outreach worker and a teacher key worker) who were appointed to the schools through the governing bodies to work full-time with parents.

The job descriptions of the staff were very broad but sought for the most part to develop work with parents as a key influence on children's learning and development in three main areas:

1 to promote the active involvement of parents in schools generally and

in their children's learning in particular;

2 to provide opportunities for parents and other adults in the community, to develop their own education in a local, supportive and informal context;

3 to liaise with a range of other community agencies across education, health and social welfare, that offered support to families.

Such was the dynamic two-way nature of the work with parents that a response was made quite early on by parents and staff alike, to rename the project 'Parent School Partnership' thus establishing the notion of working together from our different roles and perspectives and rejecting the idea of one way support as patronising and unrealistic.

Over the next five years the number of schools who were part of the scheme increased to 31 and included 28 primary schools, one nursery school, one secondary school and the English Language Centre. This centre has developed more recently into the Bilingual Development Service and Consultancy and now employs through the LEA, its own team of home–school pastoral workers.

The PSP scheme had, as now, a full time Project Officer/coordinator and linked to the central LEA structure through a liaison/steering committee comprising officers, headteachers, staff representatives and advisers. The project was evaluated in the early stages by an evaluator based at the University of Liverpool. This person was also a member of the liaison group.

Although participating schools worked within a broad consensus of aims, each school developed with parents its own programme of work influenced by its own community needs. Even though all staff met regularly as a team to share ideas and address staff issues, the organisation was very fluid. However, it enabled a creative exploration of issues to develop between staff and users. It did mean though that some purposes were overwhelmed by this release of 'creative energy' particularly the aim to relate to other primary schools not included in the programme. This aim was largely constrained by the uptake from the target groups in the base schools.

PSP came to have an identity of its own within the project schools, separate and somewhat marginalised from other schools, and viewed with some longing by the many other schools in Liverpool who did not have the same access to PSP resources, but who as a result of the benefits being attributed to the PSP scheme and to the increasing obligations on all schools to work more closely with parents, wanted to develop their own home–school programmes.

Some measure of the success of the PSP work was documented in a major evaluation exercise in 1990 with a sample of 486 users. This information was shared extensively with politicians, colleagues in FE, HE, Adult and Community Education and with other parents and schools city wide. The evaluation exercise was a key stage in PSP's development and helped raise the profile of parental education in Liverpool.

1990 evaluation process

The decision to evaluate the initiative was the result of three outside influences:

1 the climate of quality and accountability;

2 an HMI verbal report (April 1990) which highlighted the need to inform parents about the Education Reform Act;

3 justification of the service to pre-empt local management of schools.

These influences led to the City Council resolving to set up a working party to 'identify good practice in the successful PSP units which can be shared with those schools without such a unit' (April 1990).

In addition PSP wished to render itself accountable by devising its own evaluation system. To facilitate this it was necessary to agree aims, review procedures and identify performance indicators in a cooperative way with users and providers. This was carried out in consultation with the Director of Education to whom the scheme reported at each stage. In September 1990 in a report to the Education Committee he stated that the proposed evaluation aimed 'to devise strategies for assessing good practice and to measure the work of individual units against these criteria and to identify ways of disseminating parent/school links to schools without PSP'.

In order to identify overall PSP aims, individual centre aims and development issues a substantial consultation process was established between LEA, PSP staff, users, schools and other providing agencies. On the basis of this model the Chair of Education complimented the PSP Project Officer on the 'framework and process for annual review ... which takes account of the views of staff and parents and establishes PSP criteria for success' (November 1990).

As a result of this consultation process several key areas of the service provision that were important to service users were identified for evaluation:

- helping children;
- links with the schools;
- links with other family agencies;
- personal development and progression of the users;
- adult education opportunities;
- access and equal opportunities;
- community involvement.

These areas correspond to Liverpool City Council's Policy for Community Education (March 1989) which has the following general aims to:

- afford opportunities to people of all ages for growth and development as individuals in response to their needs and as members of communities, and to encourage local people to take a responsibility for their own lives;
- stimulate people of all ages and provide a continuous educational opportunity for the whole community;
- promote learning as a life-long activity, using education in the widest sense, as a means of personal and community development.

They also, more recently, correspond to the LEA's 'Learning to Regenerate' strategy (1995).

The consultation process was followed up with a city-wide users questionnaire which was administered to 486 respondents and a large-scale structured interview held with 45 volunteers.

The questionnaire compiled by staff in consultation with parents was concerned with factual information (*see* Table 7.1).

Table 7.1

Frequency of use	Reasons for attending
Adult education activities	Progression routes
Links with the school	Parental involvement through PSP
Helping the child	Qualities and competencies gained
Information gained	Contact with agencies
Community activities	Personal contributions to PSP

The in-depth structured interview with parents was concerned with open-ended informal data collection about a number of topics (*see* Table 7.2).

Table 7.2

Access	Barriers
Own school experience	Personal details
Links with schools	Links with adult educational establishments
Links with non-educational agencies	Pre-school and creche experience
Governors	Changes in attitude to education
Progression and personal development	Social fabric

The resulting data was useful in' informing the following: adult education progression routes, the development of individual users, the role of parents in education, the accreditation of learning outcomes and prior learning, staff development and the value of a supportive family service. Acknowledgement was also made of the formal and informal curricula in PSP and the various advice and guidance roles that PSP performs. The data, along with other local and national priorities also informed the annual development plan for PSP centres.

Some outcomes of this evaluation had significant impact and many lessons were there for schools and providers of post-sixteen opportunities to listen to and learn from. Recorded quotes from parents are significant:

'Children thrive if they can see a partnership rather than conflict.'
'I hated school … now I'm at ease in school, my attitude has rubbed off on my children.'
'I'm confident enough to be actually of use in the school. The shoe is now on the other foot and I feel I contribute a lot.'
'J. came on more since he sees me in school. He's good on the computer, he knows his colours and he can count smashing now.'

In fact half the PSP users whose views were surveyed recorded improvement in their children such as improved academic skills, social skills, happiness, social contacts, encouragement and cooperation. One-quarter of parents were more aware of the infrastructure of schools.

'I know how the school system works, what's what.'
'I'd like to know exactly how they're getting on within their age group, ahead or behind and their behaviour.'

But tellingly a third of parents talked about enjoyment.

'I love being in school and knowing their teacher.'
'My children enjoy coming to school knowing I'm there.'
'We have fun and enjoyment together.'

Many parents often coping in difficult inner city situations commented on the effects PSP provision had had on them as individuals.

'When you get to know yourself you see people as they really are: your confidence has grown and you're no longer dependent.'
'Opportunity to meet other parents in the same situation. Very supportive, share anxieties.'

Users recorded that they follow a range of traditional adult education courses and 53 per cent had accessed further education opportunities through PSP. However, increased confidence (a hallmark of 80 per cent of PSP users) results in a high involvement in a number of action-based projects such as community magazine production, campaigns to address problems in the local area and problem sharing in schools, as for example those resulting from school reorganisation. Even though 40 per cent of parents were unemployed positive outcomes were reported. These result in each user having an average of four involvements in their local community.

Such confidence building regarding progression opportunities is commented on by the former Director, Educational Guidance and Progression, Liverpool John Moores University:

> Progression routes for women returning to learning of any type will be much more complex in their development. Such routes will, to a large extent, reflect the rate of women's increase in confidence as a result of participation in team work, in creative activity and appreciation of the learning process, both for their children and subsequently for themselves.
>
> (Lambert, 1994)

To capture and evidence such a process so relevant to our work, PSP is developing a coherent Record of Achievement approach with individual service users and with staff from each PSP centre. This process will act as a vehicle with both users and staff, for target setting and planning, for review, for effective implementation, for quality assurance procedures and importantly for celebrating achievement and developing confidence.

So, it was clear to us that ten years on, after a major review of our provision, where many examples of effective practice were highlighted by parents having had a voice in the review process, we were poised to move into a new phase of development towards a *city-wide service,* a service that could be accessed by all schools and parents, a service that would disseminate "good practice" and share more equitably the resources and expertise that were available.

A number of other factors influenced this important stage in PSP's development and evolution.

- On time expiry of the government's Inner City Partnership support, PSP was absorbed into the schools' section of the LEA mainstream education budget.
- In the event of LMS, PSP staff although still based in schools, were not part of the formula funding which was calculated on the number of children not parents in school. The LEA consequently made a commitment to maintain the PSP as a central service. The weight of a supportive HMI report and the benefits the publicity of our own evaluation probably influenced this decision. This decision, though, had implications for PSP's accountability and its potential for accessibility to a much wider range of schools than before.
- Requirements of the National Curriculum placed obligations on all schools to work with parents. ERA afforded entitlements to all parents

to have a greater say in, and access to, their school resulting in an interest in and demand for support from a wider range of schools.

- The Education Committee after the HMI Report resolved that the service expertise and experience should be disseminated more widely and that PSP bring forward a five-year strategic plan for its long-term development as a city-wide service. This was particularly significant in respect of centralised funding to the project on the introduction of LMS.

PSP's response

As requested by the Education Committee a five-year strategic plan was submitted and subsequently approved. This set at its core a policy of LEA commitment and intent that would support existing practice and recommend further development. A small team of teachers, headteachers and PSP staff met to work on discussion papers towards the 'Liverpool Policy on Parental Involvement in Education'. Such a policy, this group believed, should reflect the experience of users as evidenced through our evaluation processes and also the effective practice that had developed over a number of years in negotiation with users and providers. As such the policy would be owned by all participants and be rooted in realistic practice. After consultation with governors and parents these draft documents were submitted to the City Council and subsequently adopted as LEA policy. A copy of the policy was sent to each school in Liverpool. The following principles were embraced within it:

- to enrich children's learning by bringing together the resources of home and school;
- to create an atmosphere in which parents feel secure and valued;
- to acknowledge and value parents as educators;
- to enhance achievement and raise expectations through a positive attitude to partnership;
- to encourage greater openness and joint involvement of parents and school managers in policy-making and the daily life of the school.

To emphasise Liverpool City Council's position on Parent School Partnership work, a statement of commitment went out to every parent in Liverpool and consisted of letters to parents from both the Chair of Education and the Director of Education and a photographic record to emphasise ways in which parents could become involved in the day-to-day life of their school, together with direct quotes from the policy as regards parents' rights and expectations.

To support the implementation of this policy, PSP staff worked with colleagues in school and in the Adult Education Service to develop two sets of guidelines that focused on a process of review and forward planning, and that addressed specific areas of work with parents. These guidelines *Guidelines for Involving Parents in Education* and *Guidelines for Involving Parents with Basic Skills Needs* were also circulated to all schools and governing bodies and formed the basis for a range of INSET work that PSP staff organised with their colleagues in school.

In this way the policy was given priority and strategies were developed through a coherent programme of staff development work for its implementation. To ensure that this work was embedded in the priorities of the school, parental involvement work was also highlighted through the Education Committee as a local priority for schools when setting their school development plans.

The setting up of the policy and guidelines also gave all the PSP staff an opportunity to assess their roles, to value and celebrate much of the good practice that was taking place and to look at the means and expertise they had to develop this into a city-wide service.

Staff were now expected, as recommended by the Education Committee, to disseminate their skills in schools which had hitherto had no support – although many were already working with parents without the extra resources and staffing which were provided in the PSP base schools. Some PSP staff welcomed this development as a release of creative energy while others felt that it was an extra work load and added responsibility to a job that already demanded more than they were able to meet. It was crucial to address the feelings and needs of the staff in this dissemination process. At every stage of development there was open and constructive discussion and many valuable ideas were fed back to the central team to inform more effective management of the dissemination and development process.

In 1991 a Development Team was set up, funded through the Urban Programme to lead forward and support the process of dissemination of PSP resources and expertise and to regenerate and develop existing successful PSP initiatives. The team which is managed through a PSP lead officer, as part of the overall PSP staffing structure, included three teacher key workers, three outreach workers based within their centres, an administration officer and a full-time, seconded teacher key worker to work from the central office, all of whom were awarded extra responsibility allowances. Through PSP planning data, areas were identified as PSP priorities and the Development Team staff took on individual responsibilities to develop these areas through training and staff development sessions, and through negotiated input into schools. All PSP staffs were encouraged to be part of this development process and by 1994 Parent School Partnership had worked with 136 schools, with a range of inputs all set within each school's own context and development plans. The areas of development responsibility of the team included:

- parental involvement in the early years;
- development/evaluation of home–school National Curriculum projects;
- parents and special educational needs provision;
- family education projects;
- inter-agency and community involvement;
- adult basic education;
- English for speakers of other languages;
- adult education provision;
- administration procedures.

All these issues were addressed in an ethos of openness, accessibility and equal opportunity which reflected a long-established culture in PSP of peer group support and involvement in taking forward staff development issues.

The Development Team met on a regular basis with the PSP lead officer to plan, review and evaluate their progress. They saw their role as one of identifying gaps, target setting, measuring achievable outcomes and of being accountable to the PSP staff, the LEA, schools and parents in the city. A comprehensive report of the PSP Development Team was produced in 1994 and circulated to elected members, a wide range of colleagues and to every school in Liverpool. This process reaffirmed our commitment to accountability and, as the report also invited schools to bid for support regarding any of the resources and initiatives contained within it, it was also used as a strategy to inform our future planning as a service striving to meet the needs of schools and parents.

Managing change issues

The PSP service is based within the Education Directorate, Community Services Division. It is managed by a lead officer, who is responsible to and supported by the head of that division. That the PSP service was a democratic structure reflecting the overall aims of the service was well established. With the extension of the service to the whole city it became important that an overall quality framework was established to demonstrate annual planning, implementation and evaluation in order to be accountable to all parties. It was from the service itself, aware of its responsibilities to its funders (i.e. the LEA) and its users that a system was devised.

Typically the service responded through a process which consulted as widely and thoroughly as possible and the current review process evolved. It was important that this process should:

- not be imposed;
- build on existing good practice;
- not involve additional work;
- incorporate additional procedures;
- be relevant to the service;
- reflect and be responsible to the variety of service activities;
- produce both quantitative and qualitative evidence;
- involve all participants in order that they should have ownership of the process.

The resulting review process (described in Figure 7.1) has evolved over a four-year period.

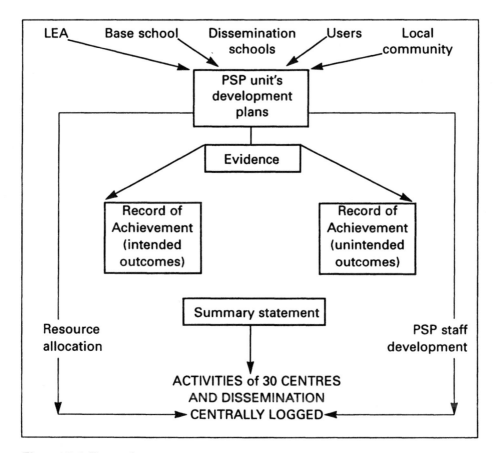

Figure 7.1 The review process

The process described in Figure 7.1 reflects the agreed procedure for review which evolved from the 1990 evaluation process. It is a refinement of the PSP unit's original development plan as a strategic document. It conforms with various quality assurance systems and aims to conform specifically with the British Standards Institute kite marking procedure.

The consultation process between LEA, users, base schools, governors, parents, teaching staff and schools who request a dissemination input is required to inform each PSP unit's development plan. This document is then given back to all interested parties and logged centrally. The development plan is also used as the basis for a PSP Record of Achievement that contains evidence of intended outcomes. Such evidence is collected to demonstrate the effectiveness (or otherwise) of the various planned activities. A range of evidence can be presented e.g. videos, photos, interviews, parents' work, children's work and course records. However, the importance of addressing unintended outcomes has been highlighted throughout and these too have a Record of Achievement in order to evidence that area of the work and to identify any general issues that may have developed.

From data gathered from our users and through the PSP planning processes PSP is able to focus its future work to provide more effectively for the adult education needs of its users in a way that places at the centre of this provision the role and needs of the student as a parent within a family, balancing a range of responsibilities and commitments. Such information can then be used to inform bids to external funding agencies over and above our mainstream budget and to ensure that the criteria of these funding bodies can be met within a context of relevance to the PSP service and its users. The issue of intergenerational transfer of skills between family members has always been of paramount importance to PSP. Through recent bids to external funders we have been able to focus on this area of concern more specifically and also meet local and national priorities for adult education developments.

Some of our bids to support specific developments have brought the PSP service into exciting and challenging new partnerships which have extended and strengthened our service base. Two examples of such developments are REACHOUT (Routes into Education through Access in the Community and the Home) a two-year part-time Access route and the Family Literacy Demonstration Programme funded through the Basic Skills Agency.

REACHOUT is a Partnership between the LEA's Parent School Partnership, the Open University (OU), Liverpool Institute of Higher Education (LIHE) and Granby Toxteth Task Force. It aims to provide an Access to HE opportunity for those students who for a variety of reasons are unable to take up a full-time course of study and who are presently under-represented in such provision. PSP provides the venue and ongoing pastoral support, LIHE provides course management and outreach lecturers and the OU has provided the open learning materials used on the course. The initiative is funded by Granby Toxteth Task Force.

Throughout the programme the domestic circumstances of the students, including the need for childcare and family support, are given particular importance. For PSP one of the important factors to be evaluated from this programme is the impact on the whole family, particularly children in school. Currently 94 students are on course many of whom had a negative experience of their own school and the first cohort are due to 'graduate' in July 1995 to take up their places at a number of HE institutions in Liverpool.

From September 1995 a REACHOUT Degree route will also be available. This innovatory initiative funded through the Employment Department brings together the same partners, LIHE, the OU and PSP. Seventy-two places are available for students in our target group to study for a part-time degree at a parent centre in their local community.

The Family Literacy Project funded through the Basic Skills Agency is an important initiative involving parents and young children in developing their literacy skills. The project offers basic skills tuition to parents but separate time is also spent with their children developing their reading and encouraging learning. Joint activities between parents and children are also built into the programme. All parents participating in the programme have the opportunity to gain national accreditation.

In Liverpool this programme has been delivered through a partnership between the City of Liverpool Community College and the PSP service, working in the context of Liverpool schools. Materials and practice developed through this programme have been very exciting and have returned to PSP, through our member of staff seconded to this project, to influence, support and redirect our work with parents who have basic skills needs.

'The future'

The service has identified the need for a second five-year major review to reflect on what has been achieved, to identify issues and to examine the changing context of the work both locally and nationally. The service will seek to demonstrate its major role in Liverpool Education Directorate's 'Adequacy of Provision Framework' to meet specific needs for community and adult education. It will also address the broader, ongoing aspects of the work such as raising standards, equal opportunities, parental involvement in curriculum, advice and guidance systems, recording, reporting, Records of Achievement, individual progression routes, family and community issues and other innovations.

The data from this review process will also inform future bids for the expansion of priority areas to build on the successful applications for additional funds PSP has already received for various ABE, Access, Higher Education and parent/child initiatives identified by the service. As such we intend to contribute to the LEA's 'Learning to Regenerate' strategy (1995).

Above all the evidence will again be used to maintain the profile of the work with a range of interested parties and to develop our commitment in Liverpool to the crucial and fundamental role of parents in education.

References

Chambers, F. (1991) 'Accountability: the Liverpool Parent School Partnership Project response', M. Ed dissertation, University of Liverpool.

Inner City Partnership Initiative (1977) *Policy of the Inner Cities,* White Paper. London: HMSO.

Lambert, P. (1994) 'Women within a Deprived Urban Community: a Liverpool case study', conference paper, Liverpool John Moores University.

Liverpool City Council (1989) *Liverpool Policy for Community Education.*

Liverpool City Council (1991a) *Liverpool Policy on Parental Involvement in Education.*

Liverpool City Council (1991b) *Guidelines for Involving Parents in Education* and *Guidelines for Involving Parents with Basic Skills Needs.*

Liverpool City Council (1994) *PSP Development Team Report.*

Liverpool City Council (1995) *Learning to Regenerate.*

Contributors

- Lyn Carey
- Teresa Cassidy
- Fiona Chamber
- Pat McCormack
- Pauline Sanderson

All the contributors are current members of the Liverpool PSP service with varying perspectives on the development of the work – as outreach worker, teacher key workers, service manager, administrator and all as member of the PSP Development Team involved in leading forward the dissemination of the service.

8 The contribution of parents to children's achievement in school: policy and practice in the London Borough of Newham

Sheila Wolfendale

In common with other chapters in this book, this chapter aims to describe a specific initiative in parental involvement in one geographical location with its own distinctive characteristics. This is an account of the evolution and adoption of a parent partnership strategy within an urban, inner city area, the London Borough of Newham in the east end of London.

The plan is to provide initial context; identify key developments impinging upon and influencing the course of events; relate the parental partnership strategy to the issue of raising children's educational achievement; discuss a number of associated concepts, such as partnership itself, empowerment and equal opportunities.

This author has been involved over a number of years with Newham's parental involvement initiatives; has been and is a member of the working party on Parents in Partnership (PIP), now the LEA strategy group, and is currently involved in evaluating part of the City Challenge and Parent Partnership Scheme (DfE–GEST funded) described in the chapter.

National influences upon local practice

The local initiatives described in this book are influenced by and in turn influence and help to determine parental involvement at national level. Likewise, a number of legislative imperatives within education continue to impact and resonate upon local practice. Local education authorities and schools have had to respond to the extension of parental rights as outlined in recent Education Acts (1988, 1992, 1993, and see Mansfield, 1994); now they have to have 'due regard to' the special educational needs Code of Practice (DfE, 1994) with its avowed commitment to parent partnership; schools anyway have to produce evidence of parental (and community) involvement as part of an OFSTED inspection. These realities have been absorbed into the L.B. Newham's overall parent partnership strategy.

Profile of the London Borough of Newham

Newham is a designated outer London Borough, with many of the characteristics of an inner borough, sited in London's East End, covering areas which include Stratford, West and East Ham and parts of the London Docklands. Its population is characterised by a particularly high proportion of young people and by great ethnic diversity – it has the second highest level of ethnic minority residents in Britain, at 42 per cent. On the government's 1993 set of deprivation indicators, Newham ranks highest (i.e. most deprived) of all the 366 Local Authority Boroughs and Districts in England. School children in Newham have for many years achieved less academically than elsewhere, and there is a proven and unsurprising link between educational attainment and Newham's poverty profile. Poverty in Newham is characterised by one of the worst levels of low income, unemployment, debt, poor housing, homelessness and poor health in Britain. This is a long-standing legacy – in 1870 the House of Commons commissioned a report into poverty in West Ham (for these statistics see Griffiths, 1994).

The Council and the Education Department have, over the years, made strenuous attempts to combat such disadvantageous circumstances on behalf of its children, and at the time of writing, the LEA remains fairly intact, with just one school having become grant-maintained. The political profile has been, and remains, overwhelmingly Labour.

Efforts to combat the destructive effects of poverty and to promote equal opportunities in an ethnically diverse area have been directed to the community and to schools – this chapter is concerned with the educational dimension. A raft of policies was formulated during the 1980s which included:

- Multi-cultural Education (1983);
- Anti-racist Education (1985);
- Non-sexist Education (1986);
- Special Education in Mainstream Schools – Inclusive Education (1987);
- Community Education (1989);
- Parents as Partners in Education (1993).

Within its midst the L.B. Newham has the Newham Parents' Centre, an innovative, grass-roots organisation which has combined a number of functions over the years since its inception during the 1970s. It has been a lobbying pressure group; it has provided training to young people and adults (specifically on the literacy front); its members have contributed significantly to education (e.g. to governor training, special educational needs, family literacy); it operates a street-level bookshop. While the NPC is in receipt of a core LEA grant, it has sought to retain its independence.

For detailed accounts of the formation, development and initiatives of the NPC, see Phillips (1989, 1992 and 1995).

Newham's detailed policy statements reflect an enduring ideology, centring upon access, entitlement and human rights, in an area in which such intervention is perceived to be a continuing need.

Tracing the evolution of 'Parents in Partnership'

The pedigree of the most recent of Newham's policies, Parents as Partners in Education, ratified in 1993, has its origins around ten years earlier. The lineage can be traced chronologically via a number of pivotal events and locally published documents and the reader will be able to discern a continuing commitment towards embracing parental and community dimensions within education.

A number of these key developments will be briefly described in sequence.

'Going Community' – community strategy

The *Going Community* document (Community Education in Newham, 1985) was the culmination, at that time, of the Education Committee's decision to promote community education in the borough. The strategy had been launched with a series of local conferences and by 1984 two community secondary schools were designated. Crucial to the thinking behind the policy was the council's commitment to equal opportunities. The strategy embraced schools, and the Youth and Community Service, and parental participation was therefore integral (Allen *et al.*, 1987). The document spelled out the parameters of the envisaged Community Education Strategy, for the ensuing years, which were to encompass all schools in time. The schools' dimension included key parental involvement activities, such as: provision of parents' rooms; participation by parents in reading; and fostering home liaison.

Community Education has continued to be a central part of Newham's educational provision, as is attested by: formulation of the 1989 Policy Statement (referred to above); the community education service which operates in three area teams within the borough and which manages a number of sub-services and initiatives for schools, community groups and adult education, provision for literacy, and of advice and information leaflets, and a regular newsletter entitled *Community Education in the School Curriculum*.

The 'Boosting Educational Achievement' Inquiry and Report 1987–88

Newham Council and LEA commissioned an independent inquiry into educational achievement within the borough, which was chaired by Seamus Hegarty, currently Director of the National Foundation for Educational Research (Hegarty, 1988). The five members of the inquiry team worked during 1987 and reported in 1988. The brief was expressed as follows: 'to increase or boost achievement amongst all pupils … through identifying factors which inhibit achievement … and identifying and developing practices and strategies which boost achievement' (p. 9).

The overall aim was to identify factors in Newham which acted as a barrier to achievement, which also drew upon research and experience elsewhere, and which could assess what could realistically be done to boost educational achievement. With hindsight the Inquiry Team acknowledged that the brief had been overly ambitious within the time-scale and resources allocated to it and that it could not do adequate justice to the complex and myriad factors that needed to be considered.

However, their data trawl (based on extensive and wide-ranging consultation, questionnaires, interviews and document analysis) yielded incomparably rich information. Comparative statistics confirmed low levels of achievement by Newham pupils in public examinations (Hegarty, 1988: 176–82). The Report's recommendations covered twelve areas, of which 'Parents and Schools' (germane to this chapter) was one.

On home–school links, the Report found 'some excellent practice, but we found too that there is much scope for improvement and that there are many opportunities still to be grasped' (p. 208). Recommendations included: that the LEA should foster home–school communication at all levels and that home–school work should assume greater importance. A number of practical measures were proposed.

The link between pupil achievement and parental participation has resonated for many years and is a recurring theme within this chapter.

The 'Parents in Partnership' Working Group

An initiative concurrent with the work of Hegarty and colleagues was the formation around 1985–86 of an interest group, which was concerned with fostering closer and more effective home–school relationships. Convened and administered by members of the Education Department, the group comprised parental and community representatives and other areas of the education service (and this author, working at the University, then Polytechnic of East London). The first couple of years or so of the existence of this group was a 'talking shop' which demonstrated, in micro, a number of the issues and tensions inherent in home–school liaison. While group members shared a 'common cause', individual perspectives and aspirations varied as to how 'partnership' could or should be achieved. Gradually, from valuable but sometimes uncomfortable discussion a number of specific, achievable goals were formulated, and group activity culminated in a number of 'products', major ones being:

1 A series of eight A4-sided leaflets for parents, covering these topics: Newham's education services; Newham's education policies; parents' rights in education; choosing a school; progress at school; concerns about your child; safety at school; employment, training and education.

These leaflets were/are also available in a number of community languages. The long process of their final production in the early part of 1992 reflected the at times differing views as to how best to communicate with parents; what 'tone' to use; how little/much information and facts to impart; precisely what use parents would make of the leaflets; how readily accessible could they be to parents. These issues reflected over-arching issues of partnership, and empowerment and the leaflets can be perceived as being intended to be just one instrument through which these key aspirations could be realised. The leaflets have been widely distributed by the LEA and the Newham Parents' Centre to schools and community outlets. Since 1992 a number of the leaflets have been re-written and published in different forms as part of the authority's advice and information for parents.

2 A parents' conference held in a school on a Saturday in February 1992: the day conference was held to: consult on the draft Parents in Partnership policy (see 3 below); launch the leaflets (see 1 above); provide a series of parents' workshops. The then chair of the Education Committee introduced the day, reinforcing the Council and LEA commitment to a policy on partnership. Conference proceedings were later written up and stand as a record of the issues and concerns raised, especially within the workshops (one of which was led by this author).

3 The production of a written policy on 'Parents in 'Partnership': the draft went to a series of consultation meetings, within the Working Group, at the conference (2 above) and to the Education Committee, which eventually in 1993 endorsed and accepted the final version as LEA/Council policy. The policy covers two sides of an A4 sheet and sets out aims and goals to realise it in practice. Space precludes reproducing it in full here – the reader is welcome to contact this author for a copy (c/o Psychology Department, University of East London, Stratford Campus, Romford Road, London, E15 4LZ).

Formation and work of the Strategy Group

At this point, during 1993, the Working Group was re-formed, initially as a small-core LEA led Policy Strategy Group, and then, during 1994, broadened once more to become broader based and better representative of parents and the community. However, the intention of the initial small-core group was first, to identify what borough-wide strategies needed to be implemented to realise the partnership goal and second, to ascertain what parental involvement initiatives were currently part of school practice. Bearing in mind the Hegarty Report observation that there was good practice but it was patchy, and not widespread, it was a reasonable supposition that, several years on, this might still be the case. In pursuance of these goals, the Strategy Group undertook two pieces of work which will be briefly described:

- survey to schools to establish a data-base of parental involvement;
- production of an Action Guide for Schools.

Schools survey: during 1993–94 a detailed questionnaire was sent to all schools, which comprised:

PART A: recent and current school practice on working with parents;
PART B: school's link with LEA policy on Parents in Partnership;
PART C: attitudes and values on Parents in Partnership.

The response rate was as follows:

Special schools: 4/4 = 100% (nb. due to the LEA Policy on Inclusive Education, special schools were and are in a process of reduction in numbers)
Nursery schools: 7/8 = 90%
Primary schools: 39/67 = 60%
Secondary schools: 8/13 = 60%

The completed returns trickled in during 1994 and so at the time of writing, survey analysis is not yet completed. The response rate is impressive, given that schools have many pressures and other demands made upon them, and the fact that the questionnaire was very detailed and called for highly reflective as well as factual responses. Preliminary analysis confirms a tremendous range of parental involvement activity, with all schools listing at least one area of home–school contact and many confirming initiatives covering: reading/literacy/maths – IMPACT, parents in school, home–school communication. Once fully analysed the results will form a sound data-base and the information can be used, comparatively, year by year, as a means of gauging progress towards the policy goals.

Production of an Action Guide for Schools (1995): this 37-page 'pack', launched in March 1995 has been the culmination of much preparatory and collaborative work, which inter-links the LEA initiative with the City

Challenge Action for Achievement Project (see below). The Guide is intended firstly, to draw together existing good practice in schools and community and secondly, to act as a stimulus for extending practice. It comprises several sections, such as 'Working in Partnership with Parents' (white pages); developing a school strategy (yellow, green, pink, blue, gold, lilac pages); transition between primary and secondary; parents' rights, OFSTED, case studies, parents' views, initiatives elsewhere in the UK, contacts, a school-based check-list (white pages).

Related home–school initiatives within the L.B. Newham

What has been described thus far represents a recurring and continuing commitment, endorsed by the Council and the LEA and enacted in a variety of ways within Newham schools. Financial backing has been essential at different stages to 'seed corn' projects, to sustain and maintain the momentum – a number of projects have been in receipt of grants from, for example, Urban Aid programme, Docklands PACT, DfE/GEST (Grants for Education and Training), and Stratford City Challenge. Of these sources, the City Challenge initiative will be singled out for brief description and discussion (below) since it represents a major funded initiative, and although the home–school part of City Challenge focuses upon primary schools/special schools and two nurseries (ten altogether) within the Stratford area, much of existing and emerging practice can be generalised to other schools.

The City Challenge Action for Achievement Project

The national government-funded City Challenge initiative is predicated on the need for 'special' funding to regenerate certain urban/inner city areas, of which Stratford is one, and as such, it is firmly within an affirmative-action, interventionist tradition. Action for Achievement has a series of targets designed to improve participation by parents and achievement by pupils over the five-year period of the project (1993–98). These targets are monitored using a common monitoring and evaluation process which is used across the projects to enable the benefits of each to be identified. Action for Achievement is being externally evaluated, as part of the wider City Challenge project and as an individual project.

Project aims include: to raise achievement through enhancing parental involvement in school; to assist parents in developing a supportive climate for learning at home; create higher expectations of parents, teachers and pupils; enhance pupil achievement in basic literacy and numeracy skills.

Targets to achieve these cover: increasing parental attendance at parents' events' initiating shared homework in literacy and numeracy; improvement in performance in English and mathematics SATs; raise teacher/parent/child expectations (of standards to be achieved); holding a conference at the end of Year 1 (1993-94).

The end-of-first year report by the Coordinator (Bawa, 1994) confirms successful achievement of a significant number of the targets by the participating schools and the parallel evaluation (Wolfendale, 1994) provides documented evidence as to parental take-up of activities on offer and their manifest enthusiasm over such participation.

Preliminary assessment of progress with targets for Year 2, 1994–95, suggests continuing and increasing take-up by parents and, in some of the settings, an evident and pervasive commitment to home–school practice. Evaluation of Year 1 included canvassing views from the project's Link Teachers (a designated teacher in each project school, released from some teaching responsibilities and fronting the project within his/her school) and participating parents. For Year 2 evaluation, views have been sought from a wider constituency of class teachers and a series of parent/child interviews. Time and again, the parents (all mothers...) have commented on how much they have learned about school routine and goals and how this greater understanding facilitates the parent–teacher and parent–child relationship (Wolfendale, 1995).

For the foreseeable future, Newham LEA plans to continue actively to implement the core Parents in Partnership policy in conjunction with externally funded initiatives focusing on specific areas such as:

- City Challenge – described above;
- the Single Regeneration Budget, targeted on another area of the borough;
- DfE Grant for Education and Training (Programme No. 24 for 1994–95 and No. 7 for 1995–96) which centres on fostering Parent Partnership in the area of special educational needs and implementing the Code of Practice;
- National Literacy Association/London Docklands Development Corporation – this three-year grant (from 1995) is to be targeted at a number of primary schools in the three London Boroughs of Newham, Southwark and Tower Hamlets, for a multimedia project aiming to enhance children's literacy achievement. Involvement of parents is integral to this project.

Appraising progress: focus on educational achievement

From this chronological account of key developments within the L.B.

Newham we can discern a number of continuities:

1 that there has been consistent commitment to parent partnership over a number of years;

2 that this commitment has been ideologically driven and predicated upon core constructs such as: human rights, access, equal opportunities;

3 that the central commitment has been reliant upon a mix of within and out of borough funding to realise policy aims and objectives;

4 that educational under-achievement by Newham's pupils has been persistent and a model of affirmative intervention involving parents has been needed to offset this.

Newham, as a case study appears, on the face of it, to conform to the classic profile of an inner city area in need of pump-priming to regenerate and 'nourish' it, environmentally and educationally. We have, in the United Kingdom, a post-Plowden Report tradition of directing government money to 'deprived' areas and Newham fulfils the criteria of need.

The link between poverty and under-achievement has been reaffirmed over many years, latterly by an OFSTED Report (1993), a National Commission on Education Briefing Paper (Barber, 1993) and by Smith and Noble (1995). These authors show that on recent achievement indices the social divide is as marked as ever and these enduring continuities are observed by Smith and Noble thus: 'the interim conclusion from data available so far must be that the inequalities in educational performance which galvanised some of the educational reforms in the 1960's are still, in the mid-1990's, as sharp as ever' (Smith and Noble, 1995: 129). These two writers spell out the deleterious effects of poverty upon educational performance, and indeed, upon *access* to educational opportunities. It appears that the supposed educational reforms (introduction of a National Curriculum, SATs, 'league tables', option to become grant-maintained, etc.) are not, in themselves, going to be sufficient firstly, to raise standards for *all* children and secondly, to narrow the achievement gaps. Smith and Noble graphically describe the 'barriers to learning' with which the (mainly) urban-disadvantaged child has to contend and list, from all the evidence, a number of requisites which can redress the balance to some extent which are:

- high quality pre-school provision;
- special reading schemes (such as Reading Recovery);
- reductions in class size for young children;
- more 'effective' schools;
- parental involvement.

'If all these were combined together into a comprehensive programme, the educational chances for children from poor families would be dramatically improved' (1995: 139).

These conclusions are in harmony with the contemporary view that a systematic or 'holistic' (some use the term 'macro') approach to raising educational achievement generally is the first requisite. That is, all the above-identified elements combine to define and identify a 'successful' school. Schools are now required to have Development Plans, and see the other requirements listed on the first page of this chapter, within each of which parental involvement is integral.

We can discern a shift over the years in expectations about attitudes to parents on the part of educationalists. Earlier (1970s) intervention projects applied an essentially 'deficit' model to the relationship between parents· and professionals. Ball *et al.* (1994) have pointed out that, within the American Head Start programme, it was assumed that 'parents would benefit from the intervention of professionals, organised the relationship on professionals' terms, and tended to see children as needing to be rescued from inadequate backgrounds' (p. 44).

While any 'affirmative action' educational/social programme targeted at areas of perceived and actual decay or blight is, by definition, predicated upon 'deficit' (always defined by using comparative criteria and statistics) nevertheless, with contemporary 'social engineering' schemes equal opportunities and parity of esteem dimensions have become driving principles. The simplistic and invidious deficit model is giving way to a model of intervention in which:

- family heritage is valued;
- parental expertise is seen as equivalent and complementary to that of professionals;
- parents, as primary carers and first educators, are perceived as cooperating partners in the educational enterprise.

This 'wealth' model assumes a value position that children are the inheritors and inhabitants of a family domain with its own rich, cultural, linguistic and domestic traditions (Wolfendale and Topping, 1995).

The L.B. Newham's range of policies, listed earlier, attest to this value position and denote a culture in which there have been genuine attempts to power-share, for example: by positively encouraging people to stand as parent governors; by having strong parental representation on key Council Committees and working parties; by working with the Newham Parents' Centre and other voluntary organisations on many educational and community initiatives.

It could always be argued by the most cynical that these efforts will always fall short of guaranteeing or bringing about 'empowerment' of parents which ultimately is a political issue. But the reader is invited to consider a definition of empowerment which suggests that any realisation of it is not solely a socio-political responsibility but a collective and educational responsibility as well.

> Educational initiatives involving parents must be perceived ... in terms of the opportunities such involvement provides for parents themselves to learn, to grow, to explore possibilities, to become familiar with organizations such as schools and local education authorities, and to become enabled and confident not only to work within these systems, but, as appropriate and where necessary, to challenge existing structures and traditions. Empowerment usually refers to the means as well as the ends of realizing and expressing wants, needs and rights and of ensuring that the parental voice is heard and has influence.
>
> (Wolfendale, 1992: 3)

The Newham schools' questionnaire returns and the case studies in the Action Guide for Schools (1995) provide eloquent testimony that, within Newham, there are many forms of empowerment, and the parental contribution is as educator, consultant, consumer, learner. The achievement dimension lies at the forefront of these initiatives, and the cooperative endeavour is summed up by two parents of children in Newham secondary schools

> i. Greater joint partnership schemes mean shared purposes in terms of outcomes.
>
> (Action Guide for Schools, 1995: 29)

> ii. How could we let you down
> You need not worry
> We will always be with you
> Worry not as we all are the
> blossoming flowers of the same plant
> We are all here expressing our feelings
> As we share similar experiences

(with grateful acknowledgements to the author, Sobia Kanwal, parent, who first wrote this poem in Urdu, and to Bopinder Samra, English Language Support Teacher)

References

Action Guide for Schools (1995) *Working in Partnership with Parents,* March, contact Bala Bawa, INSEC, The Credon Centre, Kirton Road, Plaistow, London E13 9DR.

Allen, G., Bastiani, J., Martin, I. and Richards, K. (eds) (1987) *Community Education, an Agenda for Educational Reform.* Milton Keynes: Open University Press.

94

Ball, C. (1994) *The Importance of Early Learning,* report, Royal Society of Arts, 8, John Adam Street, London WC2N 6E2.

Barber, M. (1993) *Raising Standards in Deprived Urban Areas,* National Commission on Education Briefing, 16, July: 344–54 Gray's Inn Road, London WC1X 8BP.

Bawa, B. (1994) *Raising Standards in Inner City Schools.* L.B. Newham Education Department.

Code of Practice on the Identification and Assessment of Special Educational Needs (1994). London: HMSO.

Community Education in Newham (1985) *Going Community.* L.B. Newham Education Department.

Griffiths, S. (1994) *Poverty on Your Doorstep, L.B. Newham Poverty Profile,* Chief Executive's Department, Newham Town Hall, East Ham, London E6 4RP.

Hegarty, S. (chair) (1988) *Boosting Educational Achievement – Report of the Independent Inquiry into Educational Achievement in the L.B. Newham.* Education Department.

Mansfield, M. (1994) *Home and School Links: practice makes perfect.* Campaign for State Education, 158 Durham Road, London SW20.

OFSTED (1993) *Access and Achievement in Urban Education.* London: HMSO.

Phillips, R. (1989) The Newham Parent's Centre: a study of parent involvement as a Community Action Contribution to Inner City Community Development', ch.7, in Wolfendale, S. (ed.) *Parental Involvement, Developing Networks between School, Home and Community.* London: Cassell.

Phillips, R. (1992) 'Newham Parent's Centre; parents as partners in education,' in Wolfendale, S. (ed.) *Empowering Parents and Teachers – Working for Children* (pp. 138–41). London: Cassell.

Phillips, R. (1995) 'An Urban Parent Strategy for Accessing Achievement in Literacy,' in Wolfendale, S. and Topping, K. (eds) *Family Involvement in Literacy – effective partnerships in education.* London: Cassell.

Smith, T. and Noble, M. (1995) *Education Divides – Poverty and Schooling in the 1990's,* Child Poverty Action Group, 1–5 Bath Street, London EC1V 9PY.

Wolfendale, S. (1992) *Empowering Parents and Teachers – Working for Children.* London: Cassell.

Wolfendale, S (1994, 1995) *City Challenge Action for Achievement Evaluation Reports,* Psychology Department, University of East London, Stratford Campus, Romford Road, London E15 4LZ.

Wolfendale, S. and Topping, K. (eds) (1995) *Family Involvement in Literacy – Effective Partnerships in Education.* London: Cassell.

9 Home–school projects: influencing long-term change

Anne Houston

Introduction

In many neighbourhoods, short-term home–school projects are established to provide the solution to a long-term problem, breaking down the barriers between home and school to ensure that parents, young people and teachers can work effectively together. In most cases the projects are working in areas of deprivation, addressing issues which have previously been unchallenged but where in fact there is most potential for change.

The context in which home–school liaison operates has been discussed in other chapters and there is no doubt that parental involvement in education is an area of increasing interest and accountability both locally and nationally.

This chapter will address the issues facing home–school projects and will give an account of the Home School Employment Partnership (HSEP) in Ferguslie Park, Paisley, which has been funded through the Urban Programme with a remit to influence change over seven years.

In Scotland, for many years, the Urban Programme has been the main funding opportunity for local projects to help disadvantaged areas. Traditionally, grants are made for a four-year period and are not renewable, although voluntary projects may apply for three-year extensions. The thinking behind Urban Programme projects is that they are challenging, innovative and provide additional support to disadvantaged areas.

> Projects are intended as new initiatives in new approaches, pilot trials or pump priming, and there is an expectation that, if successful, they will be taken over into mainstream funding at the end of the four year period. They are, therefore, short-term and frequently changing.
>
> (Nisbet and Watt, 1994: 26)

Ferguslie Park in Paisley, has been designated an area of urban deprivation for many years and the severity of these difficulties is quite clearly highlighted by the level of resourcing provided by local and national government recently. The aim of this input is to tackle the key influences damaging the economic life of the community. In 1988 unemployment in the area was 40 per cent and low educational attainment among school leavers was recognised as an important contributory factor.

The Home–School Employment Partnership (HSEP)

The HSEP, set up in 1991, is part of an overall strategy, funded by the government's Urban Programme, to support the economic and social regeneration of Ferguslie Park and Shortroods in Paisley.

> The overall aims of the project are to establish closer links between home and school ... encouraging parental involvement in and commitment to their children's education, achievement and employability; and to enhance the self esteem of families living in an area recognised to have particularly difficult circumstances.
>
> (Summary from the application made by
> Strathclyde Regional Council to the Urban Programme)

There are four multi-agency partnerships in Scotland, including the Ferguslie Park Partnership. These were established following the 1988 White Paper, *New Life for Urban Scotland*. Similar initiatives in England have been pursued through the government's 'Action for Cities' programme.

Addressing disadvantage has been at the forefront of the work of Strathclyde Regional Council for many years. The social strategy is a major part of council policies which are designed to ensure that those who are disadvantaged benefit from regional council services. This strategy underpins the work of the education department in specifically addressing disadvantage. In Ferguslie Park an education strategy was developed and HSEP is a significant part of this.

Although education was not originally high on the Ferguslie Park Partnership's list of priorities, this situation was reversed when the Urban Programme broke with tradition and granted seven-years funding to the Home School Employment Partnership (HSEP) in June 1991. There had been fairly extensive consultation with community representatives and schools prior to the project's inception. However, there appeared to be certain reservations on the part of community representatives as to whether HSEP staff would be accepted in the community. Much of this appeared to be as a result of 'project overkill' from years of external funding.

In June 1991, a multidisciplinary team of fifteen staff from community education, teaching, social work, careers and pre-five backgrounds began working in HSEP. The aim of the project was to improve the educational attainment of young people from the area by improving relationships between home and school and to support young people entering further education, employment or training.

The population of Ferguslie Park in 1994 was 6,000, around one-third of these below the age of sixteen. The HSEP team works with three secondary schools, seven primary schools and four pre-five establishments, and has links with four schools for children with special educational needs. The team works with families with children at every stage of education, from pre-five to post-sixteen. This necessitates the team carrying out home visits, working in pre-five, primary and secondary establishments and liaising with employers and other relevant agencies. It was the first time that a project had been developed which covered home, school and employment.

Expectations

Often one of the crippling factors in urban programme projects is the unrealistic expectations which it either finds itself lumbered with or establishes itself! There is often a temptation in the early stages of a project to agree to inappropriate pieces of work in order to establish contact with people and sometimes placate them!

The other extreme, which HSEP found itself in, was that high expectations had been built up prior to the establishment of the project and these expectations were difficult to dissect and break down. Obviously establishing early, realistic expectations about what can be achieved is crucial and it is important to try and avoid these traps. In establishing realistic expectations it might be useful to consider the following points:

- take 'time out' in the early stages to consider initial priorities (although these may change);
- be aware of others' expectations of you and involve them in discussions;
- take advice from other projects or similar ventures;
- resist the temptation to rush into initiatives to please people or yourself;
- establish clear, written 'guidelines' about what can be expected.

It was clear from the very beginning of HSEP that the expectations of it were huge and it was equally clear that it was unlikely to secure mainstream funding because of the scale of the funding (2.5 million over seven-years) and the relatively small geographical area it covered. Therefore, a seven-year strategy had to be developed which would address all the relevant issues but without encouraging such a dependency that parents, teachers and pupils would feel 'suicidal' if the project finished.

Raising educational attainment is at the heart of the work for HSEP. The concept of partnership is also central to the HSEP philosophy and practice; and a key strategy of the HSEP is the development of closer liaison and productive communication between home and school.

Influencing change

The key issue of *influencing long-term and lasting change* was one which HSEP had to respond to at an early stage and from initial team discussions, a number of principles of operation were developed:

- change must be a gradual process achieved predominantly through changing attitudes;
- dependency of either parents or schools on the projects would not be encouraged, however great the need to feel 'wanted';
- it was important not to be protective of particular areas of work e.g. home visiting, recognising the skills, enthusiasm and initiative of others;
- as far as possible, all groupwork or pilot projects would take place on a collaborative basis enabling the sharing of knowledge, skills and expertise;
- a seven-year development plan would be constructed in consultation with all other partners;
- the evaluation of the projects would begin in Year 1 and continue throughout;
- staff development and training would be a high priority;
- home visits and community involvement would take place on a voluntary basis and with a sensitive approach.

Therefore, the process of 'mainstreaming' the work of HSEP began at the very beginning of the project with the adoption of these few basic principles.

Reference has been made in a previous chapter to 'mainstreaming' or 'embedding' practice and in this context it has been to ensure that the collaborative structures developed to work with parents, teachers, pupils and employers endure beyond the life of the project.

The main objective of the project, however, was to influence change, in particular, to how the education system responds to families who may be experiencing difficulties with the education system or whose children might be underachieving within the system.

If we constantly remind ourselves that educational change is a learning experience for the adults involved (teachers, administrators, parents etc) as well as for children, we will be going a long way in understanding the dynamics of change.

(Fullan, 1991: 213)

One of the challenges associated with the external funding of home–school projects is how to influence change without appearing to threaten the status quo or in some way criticise what has gone on before the existence of the project. Why tackle the difficult task of influencing change and highlighting challenging issues when, in fact, it is easier and more comfortable to conform and become a much needed part of the (school) support system?

Using challenging behaviour is difficult at the best of times and often it is easier to be seen to be 'nice' to people as an underhand way of influencing change. This, however, cannot last indefinitely before the fixed smile turns to frustration and change seems further away than before. In fact, in my experience, the concept of partnership probably sits on a continuum which has hostility at the beginning, partnership at the end with manipulation and social engineering somewhere in between.

Hostility———►Manipulation———►Social engineering———►Partnership

A more difficult area for projects is when the issues are of both local and national significance, particularly those of a political nature. The Community Development Project (CDP) experiences of the 1970s serve as evidence that projects which start out as innovative with a remit to influence change can quickly become a threat to existing authority.

Apart from the basic principles which HSEP developed at the beginning of the project, there were three concepts which directed the work of the project in its attempts to integrate its work into mainstream provision:

- long-term evolutionary planning;
- collaboration and partnership;
- monitoring and evaluation.

Long-term evolutionary planning

It is impossible to underestimate how important the seven years of funding have been to the development of HSEP. It has allowed the project to avoid many of the difficulties faced through short-term funding.

Continuity of staff has perhaps been one of the greatest benefits, with only two of the twelve project staff moving on since the projects inception three-and-a-half years ago. In terms of team development and continuity of provision within the community, this has been invaluable.

The most important aspect of the long-term funding, however, has been the opportunity to develop a long-term strategy which allows for a gradual transfer of skills and responsibilities between project, schools and parents. 'Leadership dominated early planning must shift to shared control with teachers and others. The control base expands as evolutionary planning unfolds' (Fullan, 1991: 109).

In Fullan an interesting analysis of the evolutionary planning process in action can also be found where Louis and Miles (1990) discuss their study of urban high schools and suggest that it is best to start small, experiment and expand the successful while contracting the less successful: 'The objective of evolutionary planning is to capitalise on the "low risk" quality of smaller scale innovation to increase certainty' (p. 211).

This describes the approach taken by HSEP of piloting small-scale pieces of work to test their suitability before extending them across the team to other schools. Many different approaches were tried with regard to home visiting, groupwork, parental support groups, attendance support, behaviour support and working with school leavers and employers. Methods of operation were constantly refined and directions clarified. In some cases pieces of work were discarded where everyone involved agreed that there was little value in pursuing a particular approach. An in-built mechanism of reflective practice assisted in this.

Fullan also considers the importance of working over a five- or six-year period to develop a 'core capacity' to process the demands of change.

Below is detailed the HSEP approach to developing this core capacity.

Year 1   Building relationships and networks. Initial home visiting at times of transition.

Year 2   Joint groupwork with schools and parents/pupils. Identification of common issues and strategies

Year 3   Formulation of joint policy documents and long-term plan for the remainder of the project. Joint projects on attendance, work shadowing and exam support.

Year 4   Joint home visiting strategy with school staff. Increased staff development and training.

Year 5   Joint 'working groups' to address specific issues, e.g. language support. Development of support and training materials.

Year 6   Begin 'withdrawal' process from direct provision. Increase focus on staff development and training. Continue 'working groups'.

Year 7   Final evaluation of project and negotiation of transition arrangements.

Collaboration and partnership

Central to the concept of influencing long-term change is the practice of working in partnership with others – and of ensuring that the structures are in place to ensure the continuation of the collaboration beyond the life of the project.

The goal of raising attainment is shared with many groups and agencies within the community, but it is shared most particularly with schools at all stages, pre-five to post-sixteen.

> The general welfare and progress of young people, which encompasses their educational development, is central to the health of any community and is a key concern for employers' groups, psychological services, careers service, parents' groups, social work and further and higher education. Therefore the HSEP aims to bring together in partnership these bodies with schools, parents and young people themselves.
>
> (Robertson, 1995: 5)

One successful approach taken by HSEP was that of work shadowing e.g. teaching staff spent a day out of school 'shadowing' a member of HSEP staff on home visits and work within the community setting. An individualised programme was established to meet the objectives of each member of staff and appropriate issues were discussed, i.e. confidentiality, prior to the day. Parents were also consulted widely over their involvement in the programme.

Work shadowing opportunities offered to staff included:

- tour of Ferguslie Park Community;
- joint home visits with HSEP worker;
- visit to community organisations e.g. Ferguslie Community Forum and Community Health Project;
- visit to Ferguslie Park Partnership – briefing on operations and strategy;
- participating in a parents workshop or group;
- visit to local primary or pre-school establishments (if appropriate);
- visit to local employers/Business Support Group members;
- visit to local community education centre or youth centre.

To date over 60 members of staff have participated in the programme and each one was asked to complete a comprehensive evaluation questionnaire. Almost all staff evaluated the day extremely highly and felt that it had given them a greater insight into the community and cultures that surround the young people.

They were asked, among other questions – *In what ways will the work shadowing experience inform/change your professional activity?*

The following responses were quite typical:

> 'I see the need to meet parents outside the school. I am thinking of offering meetings in the community to parents of incoming S1 pupils re: homework help etc.'

'It is refreshing to know that education is high on the list of priorities of parents and agencies in the community.'

'I am more aware of parents' attitudes. Parents expressed a desire to be more involved and have easier access to the school. I have already acted on this.'

'Clearer idea of home circumstances of pupils – I will approach certain aspects of my relationship with them differently.'

Parents and pupils also value teachers from the school coming to visit them:

'I am a very busy housewife and sometimes I don't have the time to go to parents' meetings so I think it is a good thing that the teachers can come to your home.' (Parent of S1 pupil after teacher's visit)

'It makes your mum feel better because she knows how you are doing.' (S1 pupil)

Scottish home–school practice appears to have a particular dimension which includes a multidisciplinary approach. This also incorporates a different emphasis on credibility which requires teachers coming out of school into the community and parents ensuring that schools are responsive to the community. A new development which HSEP are planning is a 'community induction' day for new staff in schools.

The dual concepts of collaboration and partnership are fundamental to home–school work and much of it is based on mutual respect and an understanding of the values held by individuals. Involvement with HSEP has always been a voluntary activity and one which has been offered to all parents, not just those who were perceived to have 'problems'.

Wolfendale points out that:

'all children and their parents should have the right of access to opportunities to participate in such projects on the fundamental premise of *entitlement*'. We can target differentially, on the same principle as that of curriculum differentiation, according to criteria identified to suit each family, and acknowledging that not all families will want or be able to take up such opportunities at any one time.

(Wolfendale, 1992: 48)

This is a fundamental principle in home–school work and one which has paid off for HSEP in terms of relationships with parents. Instead of the stigma which is often attached when a 'professional' person comes to your home, HSEP offer their service to all parents and have therefore had almost a 100 per cent take up rate. In fact it has almost become a status symbol having a HSEP worker!

While collaboration and partnership are key concepts in home–school work, they pose a particular difficulty when it comes to evaluating the effectiveness of the work.

Monitoring and evaluation

Like all Urban Programme projects, the HSEP is accountable to its funders in local and central government. Generally, however, the restrictions of short-term funding have meant there has been a shortage of in-depth evaluations taking place on Urban Programme projects. Indeed, in many cases the evaluation takes place prior to the evaluation visit which will decide the future funding of the project. I don't think it's an exaggeration to say that for many projects the ultimate goal from day one has been to secure mainstream funding! While it is clear that this is an expectation it tells us little about whether the projects influenced any real and lasting change in the course of their funding.

A key theme of the work of HSEP has been that of reflective practice summative evaluation. Due to the seven years of funding granted to HSEP it was possible to develop a process of continuous evaluation from the beginning of the project with the assistance of Strathclyde Regional Council's Quality Assurance Unit in the Education Department and the Quality in Education Unit of Strathclyde University.

John Davis (in Bastiani, 1988) discusses the evaluation of home–school practice in the Liverpool Parent School Partnership (PSP) and talks about the need to provide 'proof' of effectiveness that could be used to justify more provision. 'There are inevitable tensions here: researchers have norms and outsiders have expectations about what evaluation is and about the kind of evidence that is needed for them to use' (p. 199).

Like the PSP, HSEP have favoured the use of qualitative and illuminative material to illustrate the work of the project. Working in partnership with others means being prepared to let others take the credit for particular pieces of work to ensure the 'ownership' of initiatives by either parents or schools. This, of course, poses difficulties when the project is required to justify its levels of funding. Therefore strategies had to devised which would balance the demand for statistics with the perceptions of HSEP's clientèle.

In the early stages of the project it was decided to record statistics on:

- numbers of home visits;
- purpose of home visits;
- outcome of home visits;
- number of pupil interviews;
- destinations of school leavers.

Statistics were already available on attainment and attendance.

Strathclyde Regional Council's Quality Assurance Unit were invited to carry out an annual evaluation of the project which involved them in individual and group interviews with partners involved with HSEP.

HSEP produce quarterly and annual reports as well as a six-monthly newsletter. In addition, some extremely valuable qualitative material was gathered as part of the project's involvement in the RAISE research project (Raising of Attainment; an investigation of support in education). The case study of HSEP was one of six undertaken as part of this research funded by the SOED. This was in fact HSEP'S first contact with the researcher who carried out the HSEP mid-term evaluation between September 1994 and April 1995.

The mid-term evaluation had a double focus – on describing HSEP work and on assessing the value of the activities to families and schools.

The evaluation was carried out as a collaborative exercise under the management of the lead officer. There were several evaluation subgroups – each looking at a different area of HSEP work and partnership with:

- parents;
- young people;
- school staff;
- community groups;
- employers;
- other agencies – social work, careers service, psychological service, community education.

Two other key areas were included:

- a study of the internal working of the HSEP itself;
- the collection and analysis of data about school attendance and examination performance.

Several methods of collecting data were used. Where the views of large groups of people were sought – parents, pupils, school staff – questionnaires were used. For smaller groups, interviews and evaluation workshops were undertaken. Use was also made of existing HSEP and Quality Assurance documents from Strathclyde Regional Council.

For the descriptive strand of the evaluation, HSEP staff provided case studies of area team activities and up-to-date summaries of team remits.

HSEP are always careful about making grand claims about improvement in any particular area of home–school work because to do that would be to deny the valuable contribution of other partners. This will be an eternal dilemma in this line of work and one which is never likely to be resolved. However, if evidence can be gathered which shows that home–school work makes an impact on people's quality of life then that should be accepted as valuable in its own right.

References

Bastiani, J. (1988) *Parents and Teachers 2 – From Policy to Practice.* London: NFER-Nelson.

Fullan, M. (1991) *The New Meaning of Educational Change.* London: Cassell.

Nisbet, J. and Watt, J. (1994) *Educational Disadvantage in Scotland – a 1990s Perspective.* Edinburgh: Scottish Community Education Council.

Robertson, P. (1995) *Partnership for Progress.* A mid-term evaluation report on the Home School Employment Partnership. Glasgow: SRC/Quality in Education Unit, Strathclyde University.

Scottish Office Education Department (1988) *New Life for Urban Scotland.* Edinburgh: HMSO.

Wolfendale, S. (1992) *Empowering Parents and Teachers: working for children.* London: Cassell.

10 Home works: shared maths and shared writing

Ruth Merttens and Alan Newland

The IMPACT project is an initiative whereby homework is utilised as a vehicle for parental participation in children's learning. Through the use of teacher-selected take-home activities, parents and children share a maths or a writing task together in the context of the home. These tasks, while school-focused to the extent that they are designed to feed into the classroom curriculum, nevertheless draw upon the resources of the home for their completion.

The influence and importance of the home context has been recognised for many years. In the USA, Canada and Britain it has been demonstrated that the socio-economic background of the home is the largest single factor in determining children's educational attainment (National Commission on Education, 1993). However, programmes such as Head Start and PACT suggest that parents' active support and involvement in children's education can make a major difference. Further, there is an increasing body of research which provides evidence of the effectiveness of the home as a learning environment, asserting that the majority of homes provide a rich source of linguistic and mathematical support for young children (Tizard and Hughes, 1984; Wells, 1986; Merttens and Vass, 1992). Projects such as IMPACT, predicated as they are upon the shared reading initiatives which preceded them (Topping and Wolfendale, 1985), depend upon the belief that the majority of children are cared for by someone who is willing to support their child's learning if regular and specific means are provided which are not unduly demanding in terms of time, resources and expertise.

Background

The IMPACT project was started in 1985 in inner London and became a major educational initiative running in three local education authorities, Barnet, Redbridge and Oxfordshire, in 1987. In 1989 the IMPACT National Network was set up and over the next three years 44 LEAs in England, Wales and Scotland joined the project. In 1992 IMPACT became a national project, and it has continued to grow as both a research and an intervention project, based at the University of North London, and working in collaboration with a commercial publisher, Scholastic Press, who have a licence to produce the IMPACT materials. In 1994, several areas in the USA and in Canada decided to implement an IMPACT programme in the schools in their regions. At the same time IMPACT, which had been focused upon maths tasks and activities, branched out into the area of children's writing. The 'Shared Writing Project' is now entering its second year and has been very successful.

How IMPACT works

It is easiest to describe the day-to-day practices and routines of a project like IMPACT through the use of two specific examples.

Firstly, a teacher was planning the arithmetic for the week with her six and seven-year-olds. She decided to send home an activity which required the children to coin-rub one of each of the coins of the realm all along the top of the page. Under each coin, they then had to draw or stick something that they could buy using only that coin. Thus, under the rubbing of the 10p, they might stick one-third of a Mars bar wrapper (in England, a Mars bar costs 30p). This proved to be quite a difficult activity since the children and their helpers had to be quite inventive to think of something costing just 1p! However, they rose to the occasion magnificently, and evidence of creative and lateral thinking was easy to see. One child had stuck a small amount of bird seed on her page, and her Mother had written, 'This is the amount of bird seed that Ben, the Budgie eats for exactly 1p!' Another had stuck one-third of a slice of bread having calculated that this was the amount of bread we get for 1p, and lots of the children had stuck the wrapper from a 'penny chew' (a piece of candy worth 1p).

When the children all brought their pieces of paper back into the classroom, the teacher had them work in groups of four or five. They calculated the amount of money you would have to spend in order to buy all the edible things on their sheets. They worked out the amount each sheet was worth in all, and discussed how much you would have if you not only had one of each possible coin, but also one of each possible note. The whole class participated in a discussion about the value of each coin and the sorts of thing you could buy with each one. Finally, the children did an exercise in their maths book calculating the amount collected if you have ten of each coin. The teacher then made a display of all the children's homework sheets along the entrance hall of the school.

Secondly, a reception class teacher (kindergarten) had sent home the following IMPACT activity:

IMPACT: SHARED MATHS HOMEWORK: IMPACT

Ask a grown-up to help you!

They must lie down on the floor!

How many spoons long are they?

Find as many spoons as you can. Lay them alongside their body, starting at their feet and ending at their head.

What do you do if you run out of spoons?

Write the number of spoons long the helper was, together with their name. Draw a picture of them.

Bring your work into school.

When the children all brought their picture and numbers into school, they discussed the numbers of spoons – what was the largest number and what was the smallest number. They drew out their numbers with coloured crayons and pinned them on a line in order. They were then encouraged to fill in the gaps – writing in the numbers which had not been drawn. They also coloured in a pre-drawn spoon, wrote the name of their helper on it and stuck it on the graph above the number representing their length in spoons. They then discussed which lengths occurred most frequently, who was the longest and who was the shortest.

One thing which made them all laugh happened when one of the children said that she couldn't find enough spoons and so she used forks. She said she had then run out of forks as well and so she had used a cork-screw! She drew forks and a corkscrew beside her spoon for the graph. Another child claimed that the 'helper' had been the cat – and he was five spoons long with his tail stretched out! The whole class discussed what you could have done if you didn't have enough spoons. Several children explained that they had used one spoon repeatedly. Some had used things that were the same length as spoons such as forks. The teacher used the opportunity afforded by this discussion to introduce the idea of a repeated and constant unit of measurement.

The shared maths activity which is sent home to all the children each week is accompanied by an IMPACT diary. This is a small book in which parents and children are encouraged to comment on how the activity went. Each activity has a line-up in the diary like the one in Figure 10.1.

Figure 10.1 Activities diary

Activity	Parent	Parent	Child	Child	Comments
	Was IMPACT	Was IMPACT	I liked IMPACT	Doing IMPACT I learned	
	● enjoyable?	● too hard?	● a lot	● a lot	
	● alright?	● just right?	● a little	● a little	
	● not much fun	● too easy?	● not much	● nothing at all	

The parents' and children's comments in these diaries are extremely illuminating. They have been the subject of a research project reported elsewhere (Merttens and Woods, 1994) and provide a measure of parents' interest and preparedness to be involved in their children's learning at the 'local' level of the acquisition of particular skills. Through the diary a mechanism is supplied whereby parents can and do make assessments of their child in relation to clearly specified mathematical skills. The diaries also provide a means of setting up and sustaining an efficient dialogue between parents and teachers over a prolonged period of time.

This dialogue results in a greatly improved discussion in the annual or bi-annual parent-teacher interviews where the child's progress is reported on and discussed. The parent, from being a passive recipient of information about the mathematical progress of the child, becomes a partner in a conversation in which both are contributing to the child's summative assessment. "He seems to be improving in his understanding of numbers above ten.", comments the teacher. "Yes, he got on much better with that 'Snakes and Ladders' game we had for IMPACT last week. He could write nearly all the numbers up to thirty-six.", the parent responds. This type of discussion exemplifies the extent to which what was traditionally a teacher monologue has been transformed into a dialogue.

The IMPACT Shared Writing Project

As was mentioned earlier, IMPACT has recently expanded from shared maths into the area of shared writing. Nine schools are currently taking part in this new initiative. Children in these pilot schools, and a series of associated schools, take home regular fortnightly activities in which:

- something is said;
- something is written;
- something is read.

As with maths IMPACT, it does not always have to be a parent who cooperates; it can be Granny or Grandpa, an auntie or a brother or sister. The results of this activity – always something written, though not always written by the child – are brought into class and used as the basis for some follow-up classwork that week. The types of activity include word games, generating lists and personal letters, poems and posters, signs and stories; tasks that require written language as a purposeful activity.

For example, one activity involves writing a greetings card to a relative or friend where both the content of the message and the written medium is a shared event between adult and child. One parent showed us how she had transcribed the collaboratively drafted message on the back of a picture postcard and urged her four-year-old to sign her name and put kiss crosses at the bottom. Another activity involved a simple word game where the child had to find the longest word they could from the breakfast cereal packet and use the word to generate a list of others. A parent and nine-year-old reported, 'This was the most fun we have had together for a very long time.'

Children at a school near Banbury were greatly entertained by the silly sentences they produced, all the words of which had to begin with the same letter. 'Sonic sat sipping sizzling Seven-up ...'. In the diary which accompanies every Shared Writing task, one parent commented that 'Beth (aged six) had trouble getting the idea, but then she enjoyed writing so much she went off and did her own sentence in the book.' Many parents also said that the activity had stimulated a great deal of writing, and most of the children's comments attested to their having 'liked it a lot'.

The parents of some of the junior children in a Witney primary complained that the task was too hard when they had to choose between three definitions of words like 'Jankar' and 'Quondom'. Would you know if the latter was 'a bicycle designed for four', a 'vegetarian dish' or a 'mathematical shape'? However, back in class the children organised a competition between the older and younger children – the younger ones won! Then the teacher explained how some definitions assumed that the given word was a verb, while others made it a noun or even an adverb or adjective. The children discussed whether there were any ways of telling which grammatical function a particular word might have. For example, 'Exponentially' they thought might be an adverb because of its 'ly' ending.

Theoretical framing

IMPACT depends on the assertion that the enhancement of children's learning can be achieved through increasing the amount and quality of parental participation. This draws on the work of Vygotsky, assuming that children come to master a new aspect of behaviour through a complex process consisting first of an external regulation of the sequence of actions or words, and then, gradually by more complex inner operations. Intellectual development, then, may be said to proceed from the external social plane to become personal mental activity by a process of internalisation. This argues a crucial importance for parental mediation and the role of instruction, 'What the child can do in co-operation today, he can do alone tomorrow' (Vygotsky, 1962). It is the involvement of the parent in what are quintessentially 'school-maths' tasks which is unusual and specifically beneficial. The parent is crucially able to provide sensitive articulation in the elaboration of the task, and therefore to enable a process of joint regulation and verbalisation which acts to increase the chances of child only or child/teacher negotiation of the same task in a school setting.

A further and interesting feature of IMPACT is the fact that, frequently, the child acts as instructor to the task-naive adult. The IMPACT process is very simple. Teachers select a task from a large bank of tried and tested materials. They discuss this task with the children as a part of the routine classwork. The children then instruct their parents in what has to be done, sharing the task at home. The task is, as was mentioned above, unashamedly a piece of 'school-mathematics', notwithstanding the fact that it may well draw upon or employ the resources of the home for its successful completion. The child is well-versed in the 'school-mathematics'. The parent is, inevitably in this respect, naive. The regulation and articulation of the task as it is elaborated in the context of the home will pass back and forth between child and parent.

Throughout the negotiation of the task, and the generation and construction of possible, probable and imagined solutions, there will be a sensitivity on the part of both participants to those aspects of the task in which the other is inexpert – 'Miss said we had to ...' and 'When you draw that line, hold the ruler further along ...'. Stories, too, are often utilised by both child and adult as a means of encapsulating a piece of situated knowledge in such a way that it becomes part of the on-going, fluid and constantly negotiated process of task-elaboration.

Some of the results of the project

It is no longer a matter for debate that a systematic programme of shared maths can be set up and sustained in primary schools in almost any area with parents of widely diverse and varied cultural and ethnic backgrounds. The success of IMPACT may be judged by considering the results of the project under the following three headings.

Response rate

The number of responses (i.e. the numbers of parents actually sharing the maths activities with their child on a regular basis) was monitored on a school-by-school and week-by-week basis in the first three years of IMPACT and we found that the rate varied according to the age of the children in the class.

- For nursery and reception children (three/four/five-year-olds) the rate averaged out at 95 per cent.
- For Year 1 to Year 3 children (six–nine-year-olds) the rate averaged out at 86 per cent.
- For Year 4 to Year 6 children (nine–eleven-year-olds) the rate averaged out at 62 per cent.

The subsequent yearly evaluations of IMPACT, as well as the various independent evaluations of the project in different areas, have substantially agreed with these figures, with no variation of more than 9 per cent either way being recorded.

What is clear is that with younger children there is an extremely good uptake by the parents of this opportunity to share maths activities with their children and that response rates of 100 per cent are not uncommon in nursery and infant classes. As the children get older, the response rate falls. What is perhaps surprising is that this lower response rate is maintained even when the children have been doing IMPACT since they were themselves infants. When we started IMPACT, we assumed that the smaller numbers of ten and eleven-year-olds doing IMPACT was related to the fact that they only started doing IMPACT as juniors, and that as the infants doing IMPACT progressed through the school, so the figures relating to the top junior classes would improve. However, this assumption has been contradicted by the evidence which strongly suggests that it is much harder to get a response rate of 85–100 per cent with this age-range, although it is commonplace in the infants.

We have found no evidence that the number of responses is directly related to the social class or the ethnic or cultural make-up of the catchment area of the school. The overwhelming factor affecting the number of responses in any one class or school is the teacher. This is a finding which emerged from the work of the pilot study on IMPACT, was replicated in the first three years of the national project (Merttens and Vass, 1992: 3) and has been corroborated further in the recent study of eight Haringey schools in an area of extreme poverty and disadvantage (DfE, 1994).

There is now a body of evidence suggesting that the numbers of families taking part in the shared maths may be substantially increased by three factors. The first is the way in which IMPACT is introduced to the parents and launched in the school. This has to do with the general prestige in which IMPACT is held, the ways in which the work done at home is valued and perceived as a necessary part of the child's work, and the overall emphasis placed upon the importance of explaining IMPACT to the parents at the beginning. The second is the use of the diaries and, in particular, the teacher's regular comments in these. The third is the building up, over a number of years, of an *expectation* that children will be reading at home every night with their parents and that they will be sharing the maths activities on a regular basis. It is this ethos of the crucial importance of parental participation which makes a difference. Schools build up reputations, and parents know that if their children go to that particular school, they are expected to help them.

Standards of mathematical performance

There is evidence to suggest that children's performance in maths is improved – in some cases quite substantially – and that their attitude to maths becomes more positive. There has been some attempt to quantify the gains to children's mathematical performance. It is clear from several reports that children particularly gain in terms of their ability to give and receive mathematical instructions, to suggest hypotheses and to make predictions, and to generalise. It has also been consistently reported by teachers that the children's mental and written numerical skills improve as well.This finding has been confirmed by the research in Haringey where the children in seven IMPACT schools were tested before and after a year-long programme of specifically number-related IMPACT activities. Each year, we receive a substantial number of teachers' and parents' reports that the children are gaining in terms of their mathematical achievement. It is clear that the volume of evidence, from both quantitive and qualitative research, has increased to the point where it becomes difficult to entertain serious doubts that a shared maths programme will enhance children's learning of maths.

The quality of teaching

Several independent reports have corroborated our own findings about the pedagogical effects of a shared maths programme (Merttens and Morgan, 1994). Throughout the first four years of IMPACT, we monitored the ways in which teachers' practices changed as a result of the imperative to follow-up the work that the children had done at home. The results can be briefly summarised as follows:

- There is a general tendency to move away from the use of individualised work-schemes and towards an approach involving group work and the incorporation of more activities of an investigative and practical nature.
- Teachers are less inclined to under-estimate particular children, or to make judgements more founded in stereotypical views of particular types of upbringing or background than on strictly mathematical criteria. Their assessments, and the level of the work they set for the child, are therefore likely to be more accurately chosen.
- The demand that the shared maths at home is discussed and followed up in the classroom leads to more class and group discussions and a concomitant raising of the general level of mathematical talk in the classroom. This also has a spin-off effect in that mathematics becomes generally a more 'visible' subject. There are frequently IMPACT assemblies, IMPACT display boards and IMPACT joint-class sessions.

The phrase 'third-person INSET' (Merttens and Vass, 1992, 1993) has been coined to explain the non-threatening nature of the introduction of IMPACT into classroom routines. The teacher and the INSET-worker are not focusing on the teacher's practice in an attempt to somehow 'improve' this. They are engaged in a joint venture, trying to get a programme of sustained parental participation in maths set up and running smoothly. Therefore changes to the teacher's practice will be negotiated and jointly constructed in an attempt to get IMPACT to work effectively. The teacher will need to discuss the maths at home, they will need to have the children work in groups to follow it up in class, and so on. The changes in teacher practices come about as a natural result of their focus on shared maths in the home.

Differences between shared maths and shared writing

Some interesting differences are emerging as we continue and extend the research work in this area. Parents do not see writing as intrinsically 'difficult', although most parents do see maths in this way. In almost all cases, the parent has a confidence that they know what writing is, that they have an image of what the product of a shared writing task should look like. In the maths, the parent frequently lacks any sense of what the finished product – if there is one – consists of. They feel ill at ease with any procedures to be used and frequently the vocabulary or terminology is new or poorly remembered from their own school days. This means that parents are more likely to 'teach' the child in the context of a writing task, and less likely in the maths. It also has repercussions for the precise mechanisms by which the activity is shared. In the maths, the child may be very much the one in control, the instructor to the task-naive adult. In the shared writing, the adult feels more ownership of the activity, and often has a more controlling input.

In a similar vein, the difference between the teacher and the parent, that is, what it is that constitutes the teacher's expertise, is almost always fairly clear in the area of maths. Teachers can do, understand and 'know' maths. Parents, on the whole, don't feel that they do. Whereas in the writing, parents feel that they *do* know what it is to write, that they can write themselves. This acts to eliminate the difference between teachers and parents in terms of subject knowledge. In asserting their professionalism then, teachers rely upon pedagogic expertise, and are more likely to make claims to possessing knowledge as to how children learn to write. In the shared writing project, we have witnessed a shift whereby the professional status of teachers is no longer maintained through the assumption of subject knowledge, but instead is sustained through the claim to pedagogic knowledge. We, the teachers, understand how children learn to write, what things are harmful – e.g. using capital letters, copy-writing or using lined paper – and what things are beneficial – e.g. encouraging emergent or developmental writing.

A related point concerns the ways in which some teachers have felt that the project will need to 'convert' parents to using developmental, emergent literacy methods and practices. In fact, parents were already indicating that they saw drawing and scribbling as part of the writing process and to be encouraged. In this sense, there was little indication of a real difference in attitude. However, the gap between teachers and parents is very real – perhaps especially in the teachers' eyes. We have recorded comments like 'She's done it wrong, using all capital letters', about a list of ingredients for a meal that a parent and child had produced. But even teachers may write lists at home that are scrawled in capitals as are most of the signs on tins and food packets. We also observed a teacher looking critically at a piece of writing that has been brought in by a child because she and her parent have used lined paper. We discussed this with the staff in this particular school, and wondered why many teachers in England are apparently convinced that children should be writing on unlined paper – possibly with a line guide. It was interesting that none of the teachers in this school had ever questioned this, perhaps trivial, practice before.

Conclusion

IMPACT has been called the most successful initiative in both parental involvement and in mathematics education of the last 20 years. While it is difficult to substantiate such a claim, and impossible to believe some of the more exaggerated claims for its effectiveness made by some of the more enthusiastic participants, nevertheless such a programme of sustained parental participation in regular teacher-selected tasks must be said to have much to commend it as a means of enhancing children's learning. But perhaps the best advocates of IMPACT are not the in-service trainers it employs, nor the teachers who are committed to it. They are the children and the parents who, week in, week out, share and enjoy working through a maths or a writing activity together. Comments about just how exciting, humorous or bizarre this can sometimes be abound. A parent commenting on a Year 6 child making a poster for a book he has read, wrote 'Simon obviously enjoyed making the poster but the task encouraged him to talk to us about his book in a way he has never done before.' And one of the teachers told us that for some of his children the IMPACT maths and the shared writing were quite simply 'the best work they do'. I was particularly impressed with the small boy, aged about seven, who stopped me as I was rushing through a school on my way to meet one of the staff. 'Hey, Miss!', he shouted. 'You're the IMPACT lady, aren't you?' I had to confess that I was. 'Well', he confided, 'Do you know what? If you start with two, and you go right on doubling it for ages and ages, *eventually* you wind up with 1,024!' He said this with immense pride and the air of one conferring a great honour on the listener by sharing this important nugget of information. But before I had time to express my admiration properly he went on, 'I learned that in bed!'

References

Bernstein, B. (1973) *Class, Codes and Control II*. London: Routledge and Kegan Paul.

Bruner, J. (1983) *Child's Talk: learning to use language*. Oxford: Oxford University Press.

DfE (1994) *Report on the Haringey IMPACT Project: raising achievement in inner city schools*. London: UNL Press.

Donaldson, M. (1978) *Children's Minds*. London: Fontana.

Grotberg, E. (1979) 'Headstart: the parental role in education and child development', in Doxiades, S. (ed.) *The Child in the World of Tomorrow*. Oxford: Pergamon.

Merttens, R. and Morgan, C. (1993) 'Parental Involvement in Mathematics: the home as a social factor', in *The Proceedings of the 1993 International Conference on Misconceptions in Science and Mathematics*. Cornell University Press.

Merttens, R. and Morgan, C. (1994) 'Parental involvement: an analysis of teachers' perceptions', *Psychology of Mathematics Education XVIII Proceedings*, 3:

303–11. Portugal: Universidad de Lisboa.

Merttens, R. and Vass, J. (1992) *Sharing Maths Cultures*. Basingstoke: Falmer Press.

Merttens, R. and Vass, J. (1993) *Partnerships in Maths: parents and schools*. Basingstoke: Falmer Press.

Merttens, R. and Woods, P. (1994) 'Learning Congruence: parental involvement in children's assessment', in *IMPACT at AERA, New Orleans 1994*. London: UNL Press.

The National Commission on Education (1993) *The Paul Hamlyn Report*.

Tizard, B. and Hughes, M. (1984) *Young Children Learning*. London: Fontana.

Topping, K. and Wolfendale, S. (1985) *Parental Involvement in Reading*. London: Croom Helm.

Vygotsky, L. (1962) *Thought and Language*, trans. Hanfmann, E. and Vaker, G. Cambridge, Mass: MIT Press.

Wells, G. (1986) *The Meaning Makers*. Sevenoaks: Hodder and Stoughton.

11 Making school more visible to parents: an evaluation of the Harbinger Video Project

Roger Hancock, with Anne O'Connor, Helen Jenner, Gavin Østmo and Geoff Sheath

Introduction

This chapter describes and evaluates a project that aimed to increase parental understanding of school through the use of video. Evaluation is seen as the 'attribution of worth' (Hamilton, 1976) – a complex process which incorporates the experiences and viewpoints of all involved in a project and is sensitive to unintended as well as intended effects. Evaluations of school-based projects sometimes lack the views of those most closely involved at the cutting face. The chapter is mindful of this shortcoming and is biased towards the inclusion of data from the school staff.

The project was based at Harbinger Primary school on the Isle of Dogs in the London Borough of Tower Hamlets and ran for two years from 1991 to 1993. The Harbinger video project was one element of a broader initiative – the Parental Involvement in the Core Curriculum (PICC) Project. The PICC Project involved a collaboration between the University of Greenwich, the City Literary Institute and a group of four Tower Hamlets schools and it harnessed resources (people, money, donations in kind and enthusiasm!) to give support to innovative home–school practice (*see* Hancock, 1994; Hancock *et al.,* 1994). Grants were received from St Katharine and Shadwell Trust, the Calouste Gulbenkian Foundation, Aldgate and Allhallows Foundation and the London Docklands Development Corporation. These helped to pay for a part-time project coordinator (Roger Hancock), running costs and certain development expenses.

Project background

In 1991, the University of Greenwich released Geoff Sheath, a lecturer in maths education, to work for half a day a week at Harbinger with the combined brief of gaining 'recent and relevant' school experience (a periodic requirement for lecturers working in teacher education) and also of exploring the use of video as a means of promoting home–school understanding. The idea of using video in this way at Harbinger came from Geoff who had particular technical expertise and experience. In recent years, there has been recognition of the potential that video holds for home–school liaison. For instance, videos have been made to encourage parents' involvement in children's reading (e.g. Blue Gate Fields Infant School, 1994), they have been made to promote the particular cultural interests of a Saturday school (Hancock, 1995), they have been recommended as a way of giving ethnic minority parents information about schools (Mortimore and Mortimore, 1990), and they have been mentioned as a way of informing parents about a school's special educational needs provision (DfE, 1994).

As part of the larger PICC Project, the Harbinger project took on certain broad whole project aims that were agreed at the outset by those involved. These included: the promotion of parental involvement in the core curriculum areas of literacy, science and maths; the establishment of a *two-way* dialogue between home and school; the exploration of ways of working in partnership with parents who speak little or no English; and the development of an approach to collaborative research which holds the possibility of further joint school and university ventures.

In addition there were certain shared 'principles of procedure' that the project team felt were essential in terms of successful project practice. For instance:

- that the parent initiatives be rooted firmly in classroom practice and 'owned' by teachers and children;
- that the project work proceed at a pace, and in such a way, which enabled all to feel 'on board';
- that the project and the school (not the parents) accept lead responsibility for making the home–school initiatives work.

Harbinger School

The school is housed in an old London 'Board School' a small distance from Canary Wharf and next to the River Thames. The neighbourhood has recently undergone rapid and striking change due to the relocation of businesses to the surrounding Docklands area. There are 283 children on roll. Traditionally, this is an area where white (English, Irish and Scottish) families were very much in the majority. Recent years have seen a steady growth in the Bangladeshi, Chinese, Caribbean and Vietnamese communities. It is possible to find evidence in the neighbourhood (e.g.

graffiti, verbal comments from children and adults) of racist attitudes towards the newly arrived groups – particularly towards Bangladeshi families, the most rapidly growing group.

The school is concerned to promote caring and understanding attitudes among the children and parents. Firstly, this is evident in the day-to-day relationships between staff, pupils and parents. A visitor senses a welcoming climate with friendly and positive exchanges. Secondly, there are many ways in which the school curriculum promotes understanding and anti-racism within the school and its community – for instance, displays of children's work highlight the variety of language and culture of the surrounding community. Thirdly, parents are made aware of the school's expectations and associated procedures when children and adults offend.

The building's interior has the classic design of a board school. All rooms have a feeling of separateness with high windows, solid walls and heavy doors. There are three floors which are reached by two stone stairways at each end of the building. Each floor has a centralised hall space with up to six classrooms leading off. In addition, there are, at various points on the stairways, small corridors leading to ante-rooms, storerooms and cupboards. It is easy for a visitor to become disoriented.

With regard to the choice of Harbinger as a project school, a seemingly biased, resource-led decision was made from the outset. The school was chosen because, through the concerted efforts of the staff, it already had quite well developed links with parents. It was felt, therefore, that there would be firm engagement with the spirit and resources of the project. In times of scarce funds and competitive bidding, grant giving bodies want their money will be put to effective use. Some parental involvement projects have fallen at the first hurdle because they select schools that 'need' their home–school relations developed and staff do not always see things in that way. Harbinger was chosen because it was a good example of what Hoyle (1975) has referred to as a 'creative school', willing to critically self-evaluate and very open to new ideas.

Helen Jenner, the headteacher, gives a flavour of this willingness in her initial reactions to the idea of a project, 'I was delighted. The school had been involved in variety of parental involvement initiatives and the regular input of an "outsider" would help us develop our work' (20.1.95). There was a similarly enthusiastic response from Gavin Østmo, the chosen class teacher:

> I was pleased to agree. I had a Year 6 class, and although I had regular contact with a number of parents, there were many who rarely came into school, least of all the top floor where our classroom was located. I felt that the project might enable me to bridge that gap.
>
> (29.1.95)

First year

During the first year of the project Geoff worked alongside Gavin to develop children's video making skills and to produce videos to be shown to parents. The choice of Year 6 arose mainly from Geoff's preference for older juniors in terms of their ability to take on the technical aspects of video making but also, as Gavin indicates above, from the school's wish for increased contact with their parents. Parental involvement becomes increasingly challenging for teachers as children move through the school system.

A number of practice videos were made by groups of children working collaboratively with Geoff and Gavin. These included, 'School Dinners – the True Story', 'Indian Dance', 'Computers at Harbinger' and 'Frogs and Toads' (the most specialised in curriculum terms). Frogs and Toads is a puzzle in which three frogs and three toads occupy six out of a line of seven squares with an empty square in the middle. The frogs and toads interchange positions by sliding into an empty space and leapfrogging each other. After solving the initial puzzle the children developed other similar puzzles and attempted to find general rules for their solutions. The video drew on these experiences and was an attempt by the children to explain to their parents what they had learnt (see Sheath, 1992, 1995). Gavin reflected on the whole experience,

> The ensuing weeks taught me an awful lot about video making, as well as actively involving the children in the project. They undertook all the story boarding, scripting and interviewing as well as all the filming. This was only really possible because of Geoff's presence.
>
> (29.1.95)

There was much that was educationally valuable and the children were very stimulated by the new and novel learning that took place. However, there was frustration about the seemingly slow pace of the project and, particularly, the time it was taking to involve parents. There were a number of good reasons for this. For instance, Geoff had very little time each week to move things on and Gavin found his ongoing classroom workload prevented him from working on the project in Geoff's absence. Additionally, a lot happened to impede the progress of a project. There were, for instance, occasions when Gavin was on an in-service course, occasions when the children went on a visit, occasions when the class needed to be involved in a school event, occasions when a student teacher needed access to the whole class – in short, occasions when the 'normal' classroom programme had to be changed in some way. Although class teaching is full of such 'interruptions' – some desirable, some less desirable, some annoying – teachers become experts at coping and skilfully maintain a sense of continuity and 'programme' for children. The cumulative effect on a project running on a shoestring of time, however, was sometimes to bring it to a grinding halt.

Consequently, it was not until the summer term 1992, that a group of Harbinger parents first saw the videos. This happened during an evening when all Year 6 parents were invited to hear the details of a forthcoming class visit to Bayeux. Many parents came so it presented a very good opportunity to show three of the videos i.e. 'Computers at Harbinger', 'Frogs and Toads' and the partly completed 'School Dinners – the True Story'. Gavin spoke about parental reaction to 'Frogs and Toads':

> The parents' responses were interesting. There were two main types. The first was that the maths in the video was very different to their own experience of maths. The second involved comments about the sophistication of our approach to maths. They were surprised by the way children used quite complicated words and language. Their responses were very positive but I think it would be good to home in on particular parents. Maybe Geoff could go and visit them in their own homes to encourage a more relaxed discussion. The parents who saw the video were a little uncertain about expressing their true feelings.
>
> (18.6.93)

Unfortunately, it was difficult to pursue this suggestion because the children moved on to their secondary schools.

Summary as at July 1992

At the end of the first year those involved in the project felt disappointed that there had not been more engagement with parents. To a large extent, the Harbinger video project had remained within the school and had not pushed, in any substantial way, towards parents and homes. This can be explained largely by the lack of time that Geoff had to work on the project (remembering also that his half day involvement covered the brief of gaining recent and relevant classroom experience *and* working on a video project). It was also due to the considerable work and time involved in enabling children to participate fully in the video making process. Helen summarised her feelings about the project to date,

> I think it's really good. I think the children have got loads from it. I think they're amazed at the professionalism of what they've done. I think it's really a pity that the amount of work that's gone into it may end up not coming to fruition unless there's some kind of continuation.
>
> (11.6.92)

The project's lack of success in reaching parents is perhaps best seen in the light of a larger professional dilemma. Teachers are contracted to work with children and not parents. Historically, this resulted in a distinct lack of contact between home and school. It is only in recent times that teachers and parents have begun to work together for children's learning. However, this very significant change has come about without official recognition of the considerable time and skill demands that this makes on teachers who are *already* fully committed to their main work with children.

The first year of the Harbinger video project saw a well-intentioned parent initiative fall short of its ambitions. It had difficulty actually reaching the parents because there was so much of worth that was going on with regard to the project *inside* school. For those pushing the project forward, this work fully justified energy and time. Helen's comment, 'I think the children have got loads from it' is testimony to the value of the classroom work. It became very difficult, therefore, for Geoff and Gavin to make the decision to tilt project resources away from this desirable teaching work to enable a more concerted lift-off towards parents. All schools have to wrestle with this resource dilemma when they set out to increase home–school contact. It is essential to have insight into this professional tension if home–school relations are to be developed.

The choice of a Year 6 class in the first year was unfortunate because they (and their parents) were not readily available for any follow-up project work. Had a younger class been chosen, extended project work could have been devised. Helen, however, spoke positively about developments to date believing that they were important if only to help clarify what the school really wanted to get out of the project.

Gavin recognised the value of video making for children but he had doubts about the place of video as an outreach means of contact with parents, especially in the older primary range. He felt it could be a rather impersonal medium and was concerned that it might be used *instead* of direct face-to-face meetings. He was, however, very enthusiastic about working alongside parents on video production.

Second year

In the second year, the Harbinger team agreed that it was important to make the project more sharply focused on parents. Two specific ideas were identified for video making.

The first idea came from Gavin and Helen and centred around 'Gorsefield', an Essex rural centre that was used for residential school journeys. Each time a group went to the Centre there were some parents who felt reluctant to let their children go. They were worried about safety and had difficulties imagining the situation and understanding the benefits for the children. Gavin therefore felt it would be very helpful to have a school Gorsefield video that highlighted the differences between rural Essex and urban Isle of Dogs and which showed parents how the Centre is run and the sorts of things that children do when they go there. One important outcome from his collaboration with Geoff was that Gavin now felt able to take on video making himself.

The video involved location filming at Gorsefield and around Harbinger school. Gavin felt he wanted to involve some children in this process but recognised the importance of moving the project on himself. During the initial stages, when he needed to train a group of Year 4 children, Geoff was able to give him support by covering his class. The video was completed by the summer term 1993, in time for a viewing by a group of parents whose children were shortly to be visiting Gorsefield. Both parents and children found the video to be very helpful in terms of supporting their thoughts about what it would be like and what children did when they stayed there. Gavin and Helen summarised their own feelings about this strand of the project:

> The video has been of lasting value as it remains a resource for each class that goes to Gorsefield, helping to allay the anxieties that parents have about their children being away from home.
>
> (Gavin Østmo, 29.1.95)

> We go to Gorsefield each year with Year 4 children and we will have our own personalised video to show parents instead of the official rural centre one. We have to work quite hard to get Bangladeshi parents to let their children go unless an older brother or sister has gone. They will see on video other Bangladeshi children who have gone to Gorsefield and who have come back safely.
>
> (Helen Jenner, 8.7.93)

The second idea for video making arose out of a suggestion from Helen who felt it would be helpful if a group of parents made a video about the school's new Early Years Unit. She had picked up concern from some parents that the integration of nursery and reception children in one educational context was problematic. She wanted to reassure them that it was socially and educationally sound and thought that a good way to do this would be actively to involve parents in video making and then to make it widely available to others.

Geoff worked closely with Anne O'Connor, head of the purpose built Unit, to recruit a small group of parents and to begin planning and filming. The seemingly straightforward plan to recruit parents was not without some difficulties. For instance, when the idea was first communicated to parents, some misunderstood the words 'become involved in making a video', assuming that they were being asked to appear in a video made by teachers. This had the effect of putting them off! Additionally, some parents lacked the confidence to volunteer believing they did not have the required technical skills. It was a reminder to staff that, in some areas of learning, parents are less confident than their children.

Eventually, however, a group came forward and, with Geoff and Anne's help, they drew up a list of questions that parents were asking about the Unit. For instance: who works in the Unit and how is it run? What are the different carpet areas for? How many children in each group? What happens when a child first starts? What happens if children wet themselves? What exactly do children do all day? Such questions provided a basis for filming the sequences in the Unit and interviewing the staff and also for producing a booklet of answers to common questions. Anne reflected on the way things had gone:

> Although many parents were interested in the outcome of the project, it was difficult gathering a group who were firstly, willing and confident enough to be involved, and secondly, able to make a time commitment. We ultimately had a core of three parents who followed the project through to the end and were credited on the video. They overcame their initial anxieties about their technical abilities and seemed to enjoy the practical experience of filming. They made positive comments about how it extended their awareness of various aspects of early years education and, in particular, how valuable play is in the learning process.
>
> (18.1.95)

The completed video 'Welcome to Harbinger Early Years Unit' (in English and Sylheti) has been very successful. It is loaned to parents and occasionally watched with them on the first home visit before children are admitted. Parents without video players still borrow it and watch it at a friend's house.

Anne continued:

> Parents speak positively about their children's reactions to the video. Typical comments include, 'She wants to watch it all the time!' 'She enjoyed everything on it – it was good.' 'Yea, he really loved it. He knew it was his sister's big school so he wanted to go too.' 'It's nice, I think it's a good idea.' Parents also tell us that they think it is informative, particularly with regard to the Unit's toilets! A Bangladeshi grandmother, when asked what she thought mimed the Makaton sign for 'Twinkle, twinkle little star' (as seen in the sequence dealing with carpet time) and said the family liked that bit the best.
>
> Many of our recent admissions are younger siblings of children featured in the video and this provides another valuable link between home and school for the very young child. The establishment of such links is not only fundamental to the successful admission of a young child but also to future parental involvement with the school and curriculum.
>
> (18.1.95)

In terms of the future use of video, although Anne saw the value of involving parents in the production process she felt that a professionally made film with annual updates would make the most effective contribution to the Unit's parental involvement programme.

Conclusion

Initiatives that aim to develop parental involvement have to enter the 'tight weave' of the school's educational setting. The extent to which projects are successful lies with the way in which they can be effectively crafted to run alongside, and contribute to, the school's prime function of teaching children (see Hancock and Gale, 1995). The Harbinger video project's main focus in the first year was training children to make videos for parents. Educationally, this was a novel and exciting idea. It was, however, very ambitious given Geoff's small amount of weekly time, the dual demands of 'recent and relevant' and project work, and Gavin's Year 6 workload. The children undoubtedly gained much from the focus but the parents gained little. The project's starting point was 'too far back' to achieve full lift-off to parents in the time available.

Unlike many projects, the Harbinger project had a second year which, as Helen said, 'enabled the fruits of a first year's experience to be realised'. Gavin's newly found video skills enabled him to work with a small group to produce the well-focused Gorsefield Video while Geoff took the class. The Early Years Unit video was similarly appropriately focused from the parents' point of view. The recruitment of parents to help plan and film it meant that it quickly became an activity that promoted parental involvement. The parents in the team learnt about the Unit *at the same time* as filming it and they were able to share this knowledge with other parents.

Finally, it is interesting to note the slightly different ways in which Gavin and Anne would want develop video in relation to parents. Gavin is left feeling impressed with the video making process and the potential that this has for parent/teacher co-working and understanding. Anne prefers to have a video made quickly and then periodically updated. Her main focus is on using video to inform the wider community of parents about the Early Years Unit not on involving them in production. The differences are very much a matter of emphasising particular aspects along the same continuum. Clearly, both perspectives are identifying an important role for video in terms of making school more visible to parents and increasing home–school understanding.

References

Blue Gate Fields Infant School (1994) *Adults and Children Reading Together,* (5 minute video). King David Lane, London E1 OEH.

DfE (Department for Education) (1994) *Code of Practice on the Identification and Assessment of Special Educational Needs.* London: DfE Publications.

Hamilton, D. (1976) *Curriculum Evaluation.* London: Open Books.

Hancock, R. (1994) *Parental Involvement in the Core Curriculum (PICC Project): summary and progress report for the period 1.9.91 – 30.6.94.* PICC Publications: 6 Chestnut Avenue, Crouch End London N8 8NY.

Hancock, R. (1995) *The Chinese Independent School of Tower Hamlets: a video about the life and learning of a Chinese Saturday School.* PICC Project, Tower Hamlets Learning Design Centre, English Street, London, E3 4TA.

Hancock, R. and Gale, S. (1995) 'Reflecting on the Experience of Promoting Home Reading Programmes', in Wolfendale, S. and Topping, K. (eds) *Family Literacy in Education: effective partnerships in education.* London: Cassell.

Hancock, R., Smith, P., Sheath, G. and Beetlestone, F. (1994) 'Getting Started on the PICC Project: preparing the ground for a project to involve parents in children's education', in Dombey, H. and Spencer, M. (eds) *First Steps Together: home–school early literacy collaboration in European schools.* IEDPE, Staffordshire: Trentham Books.

Hoyle, E. (1975) 'The creativity of the school in Britain', in Harris, A., Lawn, M., and Prescott, W. (eds) *Curriculum Innovation.* London: Croom Helm.

Mortimore, P. and Mortimore, J. (1990) 'Report on Consultancy Concerning the Teaching of English to Pupils in the Borough of Tower Hamlets', in Sofer, A. and Jenkins, V. *Learning English.* Tower Hamlets Education Authority.

Sheath, G. (1992) *Parental Involvement in the Core Curriculum at Harbinger School* (20-minute video). School of Primary and Secondary Education, the University of Greenwich, Avery Hill Campus, Bexley Road London SE9 2PQ.

Sheath, G. (1995) 'Children Making Maths Videos: how making videos can aid children's mathematical communication and reflection', in Burton, L. and Jaworski, B. (eds) *Technology in Mathematics Teaching – a Bridge between Teaching and Learning.* Bromley: Chartwell Bratt.

12 Setting up a parents' advice centre: partnership or PR?

Sarah Gale

This chapter explores some of the issues involved in establishing an advice centre for parents of children with special educational needs in one inner London borough, Tower Hamlets. It looks at the developments, both nationally and locally, which have supported this venture, but it also tries to identify the inherent tensions and sometimes conflicting philosophies which underpin the rather nebulous concept of partnership with parents in the educational arena post ERA (Education Reform Act, 1988). Finally, there is a review of what has been achieved in the first year of the centre's existence and an attempt to chart the likely future course of the project.

Why create an advice centre?

There were two key influences on local thinking: the first was the ACE (Advisory Centre for Education)/University of Lancaster Research Project, 'Bangladeshi parents and education in Tower Hamlets' (Tomlinson and Hutchison, 1991), which sought to explore Bangladeshi parents' views of and levels of knowledge about the education service. The second was the report of an external consultant, David Galloway (Galloway, 1990), which reviewed provision for children and young people with special educational needs. This survey was carried out at much the same time as the ACE research (early 1990) and the report aimed to inform decision-making at the point when Tower Hamlets Council took over responsibility for education in the borough from the much larger ILEA (Inner London Education Authority), abolished in April 1990.

Both reports highlighted the fact that Bangladeshi parents (current statistics show that 51 per cent of all primary school pupils in Tower Hamlets are of Bangladeshi origin) are seriously disadvantaged not only by their socio-economic position, but also by their lack of knowledge about the English education system, many parents having had no personal experience of attending schools in this country. Add to this low levels of parental education (32 per cent of mothers and 19 per cent of fathers in the ACE research sample had no schooling at all) and lack of English, particularly among mothers, and it is not surprising that home–school contact and interaction are sometimes difficult to achieve. The ACE report noted that many parents 'have to struggle to understand the complexities of curriculum, teaching methods, school organisation and educational change' (Tomlinson and Hutchison, 1991: 43). This lack of knowledge means that they are less likely to become involved in their children's education or, as Galloway pointed out, to assert their new rights under educational legislation.

Focusing more closely on parents' experience of the statutory assessment process, Galloway was very clear about the shortcomings of the system:

> All too often parents see the road to access to special provision as an extended minefield. LEA officers and educational psychologists, who are usually trying to share information and give advice in a constructive and sensitive way, can all too easily be seen as obstructive or hostile.
>
> (Galloway, 1990: 153)

Galloway went on to argue that although the borough had policies in place for informing parents about the full assessment procedures and their rights to make representations or to appeal, parents really need to know what questions to ask before they can understand the part they can play in their child's assessment.

In fact, although Galloway saw the local education authority's procedures as being more 'parent-friendly' than in many other LEAs, and noted that cultural issues were recognised when assessing bilingual pupils, he recommended that Tower Hamlets should consider funding an independent advisory service for parents whose children are undergoing statutory assessment. He saw this as being necessary because of the conflict between the professionals' role as child/parent advocates during the assessment (particularly true of educational psychologists) and their role as employees of the LEA, with views constrained by LEA policies, especially on provision. He argued that the work of this service should be monitored independently on an annual basis.

The underlying philosophy behind both the ACE and Galloway reports, although not always stated explicitly, is the notion of community participation and empowerment of parents, i.e. the need to give parents a voice and to raise awareness of parental rights. The ACE report refers to the Education Acts of the 1980s, which gave parents more legal rights to choice of school, to increased representation on governing bodies and to more information from schools, but it emphasises that parents 'also have democratic rights as co-educators, co-clients and as tax-payers, to be involved in decisions about education' (ACE, 1991: 2).

Resting as it does on pluralist assumptions about groups competing openly for access to power, the concept of community participation in decision-making, however illusory it may be, has dominated thinking about relationships between home and school since the late 1960s. It was clearly responsible for the growth of 'education shops' and LEA sponsored advice centres, modelled on the pioneering work of the Advisory Centre for Education. Interestingly, this organisation, which initially started out in 1960 as a middle-class, consumerist service, helping parents to make informed choices about their children's education, has only achieved its wider reputation as a campaigning pressure group in recent years.

In fact, it is this notion of parents as demanding consumers rather than participants in the education system that has been pushed by DES and DfE publications (DES, 1991; DES, 1992 and DfE, 1994a) and in a series of government pronouncements. The rise of the 'New Right' with its espousal of consumer sovereignty and individualism has led to much greater emphasis on parental access to power through the operation of consumer choice, rather than collective action. In reality, the choices open to parents may be very limited and restricted to choosing to remove a child from a school or voting for the school that their child attends to opt out of local authority control. So while the concept of partnership may be promoted in government literature, it is parent power which is encouraged as the real vehicle for reducing the power of LEAs and thus strengthening central government (DES, 1992).

By contrast, the Code of Practice on the identification and assessment of special educational needs (DfE, 1994b) appears to represent a less confrontational relationship between home and school, with its emphasis on collaboration to tackle children's difficulties, whatever their cause:

> The school-based stages should therefore utilise parents' own distinctive knowledge and skills and contribute to parents' own understanding of how best to help their child ... the most effective provision will be made when they are open and confident in **working in partnership** with the school and with professionals.
>
> (para. 2:29)

Sandow (1995) argues that the Code of Practice may, in fact, redirect parental energies away from the consumer model and confrontation. She contrasts the emphasis on the active involvement of parents in their child's education found in the Code of Practice with the tone of disagreement, dissatisfaction and complaint which dominates the Parents' Charter (DES, 1991). Therefore, although increasingly disillusioned by the prevailing view of parent power as a vehicle for government-led, centralist change, it may be that schools and LEAs will be encouraged to see the Code of Practice as reconciling the old goal of parent empowerment with the new demands of recent legislation.

This then was the context for the creation of a parents' advice centre in

Tower Hamlets. Not only was it hoped that it would be proactive in increasing parental participation in decision-making about children's special educational needs, but it also aimed to improve parental access to information upon which to base choices, as recommended by both the ACE and Galloway reports. A key element in this would be access to parent support networks and direct help in understanding the complex, bureaucratic statutory assessment procedures.

The feasibility study

A detailed feasibility study was carried out (Hancock, 1993) and a range of voluntary groups, parents and professionals was consulted. This study recommended the creation of a parents' advice centre, but – with no obvious source of funding – a support-line, operated by a team of parents (paid) and teachers was seen as offering a realistic starting point. However, the study also stressed the importance of providing a room where parents could meet, opportunities for workshops and the formation of self-help groups.

In fact, the completion of the feasibility study coincided with the announcement of new government funding through GEST (Grants for Education Support and Training) for the development of SEN parent partnership schemes over a three-year period. In the first year the objectives were 'to encourage parental partnership, to reduce conflict and to minimise the number of statutory appeals over the LEA processes of identifying, assessing and making statements for pupils with SEN' by assisting LEAs to foster the development of parent information and advisory services. There was an emphasis on the need to make effective links with existing local or national voluntary groups and organisations offering advice and services to parents.

The most contentious aspect of the scheme was, arguably, the requirement to show how the LEA's proposed plan would lead to a reduction in the number of statutory appeals (a key performance indicator). At first glance this seems logical enough, as a low number of appeals should reflect customer satisfaction. In other words, the education system is shown to be responding sensitively and efficiently to consumer demand. However, where parental knowledge and understanding of the education system is limited, parents may lack the confidence to challenge decisions reached largely by professionals. If this is the case, it could well be argued that a low number of appeals simply reflects parental lack of information. Paradoxically, a more positive performance indicator for an LEA such as Tower Hamlets, might be an increase in the number of appeals! Again, the concept of partnership and the underpinning philosophy require clearer definition.

Conflicting philosophies

This lack of clarity about philosophy has been well-explored in a recent study of a parents' centre established in a neighbouring borough (Vincent, 1993). This study demonstrates how moves to introduce participatory processes may be motivated by a need to legitimate the institution concerned, in this case the local authority. With rhetoric typical of such enterprises, it was claimed that the centre would 'make a reality of the concept of a partnership between the education service and parents'. Vincent argues that the very vagueness of the term 'partnership' in this context provides symbolic reassurance, as it 'condenses' emotions into a word which has positive connotations for everyone. This enables the term to gather assumed meanings about which there is apparent agreement, while in reality the various interested parties involved in the setting up of the centre (LEA, schools, parents, parent volunteers and advice workers) interpreted the aims somewhat differently. The Education Directorate actually saw the Parents' Centre primarily as a channel of communication between the LEA and parents, i.e. fulfilling a public relations function.

By contrast, another neighbour, the Newham Parents Centre (established by parents in 1973 and run by an independent management committee), gives a key role to parents. Ray Phillips, Director of the Newham Parents' Centre, argued that the success of the developing educational partnership in Newham was due to

> close collaboration between the 'laity' and professionals built on mutual respect. As non-professionals, parents have been encouraged to shed the traditionally passive 'client' role for that of active partner. Responsibility has been taken for the initiation and execution of ambitious educational programmes.
>
> (Phillips, 1989: 103).

Although the Tower Hamlets Parents' Advice Centre does not have an independent management committee, there is an advisory committee made up of centre users (parents, parent groups and voluntary organisations) and this meets regularly to receive reports on progress from the paid workers, to discuss issues that have arisen and make suggestions about future policy. A current concern is the need to establish an SEN Parents' Forum so that parent views can reach the SEN Strategy Group in a more formalised way. It is hoped that this will facilitate two-way consultation on a range of issues and will give parents a stronger voice at policy-making level.

The GEST funding covers the salaries of three bilingual Bengali/Sylheti-speaking advice workers, with a part-time project manager seconded from the SEN Support for Learning Service. This means that there is a clear separation of the management of the centre from the SEN administration and the professionals involved in identifying and assessing children with special educational needs, making it possible for the centre staff to retain some distance from both schools and LEA officers. At the same time, however, ease of contact with LEA personnel and systems has enabled them to access information quickly and to tap into borough networks, for example to obtain parent representation on borough working parties. There has been no attempt to pretend that the centre is independent, but neither has there been any pressure from the authority for the centre to develop a public relations role.

Responding to local needs

In setting up the parent partnership scheme, a key consideration was the number of parents for whom English is a second language, since these families find it particularly difficult to access information and support from national voluntary organisations, as highlighted by earlier reports. In fact, one of the first tasks of the new team was to make contact with any existing groups in the borough working to support parents of children with special educational needs. It soon became obvious that very few of the national organisations had local branches (MENCAP and Barnado's were the exceptions) and there was an immediate need to help parents to set up groups to fill gaps in the support networks.

One of the advice workers had developed strong links with the parents of deaf and hearing-impaired children through her support work at the weekly signing class, held to help parents communicate with their children at home. These parents were anxious to fundraise to enable the group to offer outings and other social events to families of children who might be very isolated from their peers because of their communication difficulties. With support from the National Deaf Children's Society, the group has adopted a constitution and elected a committee and is now established as the Tower Hamlets Deaf Children's Society. Regular meetings are held at the Parents' Advice Centre and there is a very popular weekly English class for parents (mainly mothers) anxious to improve their English. The group is also keen to establish after-school clubs run by parents.

Using this successful model, the aim is to set up further support groups, some of a more generic nature. The Early Years Development Officer from the national MENCAP office, for example, ran a very successful one-day-a-week course over one term which was targeted at parents of young children with a disability. One of the Parents' Advice Centre team acted as interpreter for the Sylheti-speaking mothers who attended.

The group members identified the areas that they wanted covered at the outset of the course and these ranged from leisure services, respite care, welfare benefits and parent rights through to dealing with challenging behaviour and stress management. Very few of the parents knew each other before the course began, but by the end of it they had decided to go on meeting regularly. Two of the parents want to set up a support group specifically for parents who, like themselves, have children who have suffered brain-injury as a result of accidents. The Parents' Advice Centre will offer them the facilities (use of rooms, photocopier, telephone etc.) to get it up and running.

Premises

What has emerged clearly during the course of the first year is that having premises which offer a clear, designated space for parents to meet has been one of the keys to encouraging parental involvement and a sense of ownership of the centre. Initially the project was based in one room in the SEN Centre, which was booked for one afternoon a week when the telephone helpline operated (as envisaged in the original feasibility study). Parents were also invited to drop in without the need for an appointment at that time, whereas during the rest of the week the workers operated an outreach service. This involved visiting parents at home or at their child's school to give support in understanding the assessment process, reading and interpreting letters, reports and documents (including the child's statement of special educational need) and helping them to record their views. Contact with the advice workers could be made directly by parents or through the school.

It soon became apparent that the room booked for drop-in sessions was in constant use for other purposes and on some occasions meetings had to take place elsewhere. Therefore the search for alternative accommodation became a priority. Again, by good fortune, a single-storey building at the rear of the SEN Centre became available. Costs for the essential building work, including the conversion of one large room into a children's crèche with an outside play area, were kept as low as possible and volunteer parents carried out all the internal redecoration.

In addition to the children's crèche and adjoining parents' room, where classes and small meetings are held, there is a further large meeting room, so that most size groups can be accommodated without difficulty. Having the facilities of the new centre has made an enormous difference to the project and parent use continues to grow daily, as information spreads by word of mouth. Many parents drop in casually without appointments and the phone seems to ring almost continuously on some days. This has affected the amount of home-visiting that the advice workers can undertake (it tends to be very time-consuming). Therefore parents are now being encouraged to come into the centre for meetings, if at all possible. This has the added benefit of introducing them to the building and making them aware of the facilities on offer.

New developments

An after-school literacy support group has just been started and this is run by teacher volunteers from the Support for Learning Service. The workshop sessions give parents practical ideas about ways that they can support their child at home, but also provide an opportunity for mutual support. An added bonus is the chance to use the computer and a range of interactive programmes accessed through CD-ROM.

A fathers' group also operates and visiting speakers lead discussions on a range of issues. Group members take a key role in deciding the issues and the form meetings will take. Another idea that is currently being piloted is the running of a regular monthly workshop for parents who have just received "the first letter" from the SEN Section (requesting permission for the LEA to begin the statutory assessment of their child). These workshops are organised with the Named Officer of the LEA, who has responsibility for liaising with parents over all arrangements relating to statutory assessment and the making of a statement. They give parents an opportunity to find out more about what is involved in the assessment and to ask questions, either individually or in a group.

A termly, dual-language newsletter keeps parents informed of forthcoming events, ongoing groups and courses, as well as news items, and this is distributed through schools. News is also put in the free newspaper published by the council and delivered to every household weekly.

One of the lengthiest tasks has been the production of a series of information leaflets about special educational needs and assessment in English and Bengali. Drafting and redrafting written information in simple, jargon-free language is not as easy as it might seem and every round of consultation throws up more changes and amendments. The final versions of the leaflets have been printed in sufficient quantities for every parent of a child with special educational needs (even at an early stage of concern) to receive a set distributed by schools (or direct) in a specially printed folder. More leaflets are planned in response to suggestions from parents and the aim is to make the collection as comprehensive as possible.

This year the criteria for the GEST bids have shifted slightly and the emphasis in the current funding cycle (1995–6) is on developing a 'Named

Person' register and training programme for volunteers who are willing to give support and advice to parents of children with special educational needs. To some extent the Parents' Advice Centre workers are fulfilling this role, but they are not independent of the LEA, as envisaged by the DfE, and would experience a conflict of loyalties if asked to assume an adversarial role as a parent advocate. Volunteers from parent groups and voluntary organisations who are prepared to act as 'befrienders' receive training in basic counselling techniques and follow a programme, delivered by ACE in the first year of the project, which gives participants a good overview of the new legislation as it relates to special educational needs. This training will be repeated for new groups of volunteers, supplemented by local knowledge and ongoing support.

One mother with many years of experience as a parent and foster parent of children with special needs helps other parents to fill in application forms for the Disability Living Allowance. Many families are entitled to this benefit, but, as with other grants, do not apply because of lack of information or confidence in dealing with the paperwork involved. Parents appreciate being supported by another parent who not only understands 'the system', but also some of the feelings and anxieties they experience. As more and more parents become involved in the centre, this form of support should grow and it will offer parents an alternative to the array of professionally run services that they will have previously encountered. Regardless of how good these are, parents inevitably retain their client status and partnership, however it is defined, remains unequal in many respects.

The future

If the new centre is to survive beyond the end of the GEST funding period (March 1997), it is essential that both users (parents) and funders (this includes the LEA) see it as having a real role to play in facilitating parental participation in decision-making, not only at an individual level, by helping parents to make informed choices about their child's education, but also by encouraging *collective* parental participation. Individually focused casework, although it may meet a pressing need, is essentially reactive and fails to address deeper rooted issues which may necessitate the support in the first place. On the other hand, the development of self-run parent support groups and active parent involvement in the Advisory Committee and SEN Parents' Forum, may result in pressure group activity which leads to an improvement in services for all parents.

However, it is important to recognise that parents are not a homogeneous group with a clearly defined set of common interests.

Experience at national level suggests that many SEN parents' groups represent the interests of particular disabilities and that their lobbying is sectional, with some categories of SEN not being formally represented at all. If this is to be avoided, there need to be clear structures in place, both at national and local level, which ensure adequate consultation and collaboration in decision-making, so that potentially disadvantaged groups are not marginalised.

Equally important is the concern to make parents feel more confident in their role as parents of children with special educational needs. The recent growth of family centres which is described by Pugh *et al.* (1994) demonstrates the importance of a continuum of help and support which such centres can provide. The aim for the Parents' Advice Centre is to create an open-access range of provision at the centre itself and, wherever possible, to help parents to make use of services offered by other agencies, statutory and non-statutory, within the borough. Alongside the client-focused casework, which in some instances may offer help over a relatively short period of time (the duration of the statutory assessment, for example), there is a mix of activities which parents can 'dip into' according to their need. However, it is crucial to recognise the expertise and 'know-how' that parents of children with special educational needs acquire, often without realising it, in the course of bringing up their own children. By giving parents the opportunity to support others and be providers of services, not just recipients, this expertise can be properly acknowledged and accessed by others.

Despite a clear commitment to work proactively to give the most disadvantaged parents a voice, it still remains to be seen how far the centre will be able to resolve the conflicting philosophy of parent empowerment, manifested in parental representation, with parent power, as expressed through consumer choice. The other imponderable question is how important the issue of independence from the LEA (or lack of it) will be to parents and whether the centre will manage to achieve the delicate balancing act of working within the system to achieve change. The real measure of the centre's success, however, will be the views of the users: if parents feel that the centre serves their needs and show this through the use they make of it, its future should be assured.

References

Advisory Centre for Education (ACE) (1991) 1b Aberdeen Studios, 22 Highbury Grove, London N5 2EA.
Department for Education (1994a) *The Parents' Charter (revised)*. London: DfE.
Department for Education (1994b) *The Code of Practice on the Identification and*

Assessment of Special Educational Needs. London: DfE.

Department of Education and Science (1991) *The Parents' Charter.* London: DES.

Department of Education and Science (1992) *Choice and Diversity.* London: HMSO.

Galloway, D. (1990) *Support for Learning in Tower Hamlets: report of the consultant in special educational needs to the chief education officer.* Lancaster: University of Lancaster.

Hancock, R. (1993) *Parent Advice Centre Feasibility Study.* Tower Hamlets Support for Learning Service, SEN Centre, Harford Street, London E1 4PY.

Phillips, R. (1989) 'The Newham Parents' Centre: a study of parent involvement as a community action contribution to inner city community development', in Wolfendale, S. (ed.) *Parental Involvement: Developing Networks between School, Home and Community.* London: Cassell.

Pugh, G., De' Ath, E. and Smith, C. (1994) *Confident Parents, Confident Children.* London: National Children's Bureau.

Sandow, S. (1995), 'Parents and Schools: developing a partnership approach to advocacy', in Garner, P. and Sandow, S. (eds) *Advocacy, Self-advocacy and Special Needs.* London: David Fulton.

Tomlinson, S. and Hutchison, S. (1991) *Bangladeshi Parents and Education in Tower Hamlets.* ACE, 1b Aberdeen Studios, 22 Highbury Grove, London N5 2EA.

Vincent, C. (1993) 'Community Participation? The establishment of "City's" Parents' Centre', *British Educational Research Journal,* 19 (3).

13 Parents and secondary schools: a different approach?

Emma Beresford and Angus Hardie

Introduction

Parents and secondary schools face a dilemma. The home is clearly a critical influence in determining how well a child will perform at school. However, the characteristics of the early years of primary school which are so conducive to active parental involvement are long gone by the time a child enters secondary school. The syllabus becomes increasingly complex and difficult for parents to understand; children begin to demand more independence from their parents; parents may want to return to work and have less time to devote to their children; there are more teachers for parents to relate to; the regular daily contact of picking up children has gone and the atmosphere and appearance of a secondary school can often be intimidating. These obstacles to a positive home–school relationship seem compounded by the fact that most of the literature and debate that surrounds this subject is also rooted in the early years of primary school.

In the absence of a definition of parental involvement and strategies which fit comfortably within the changed circumstances of secondary education, teachers and parents are left to wrestle with ill-fitting notions of the 'supportive parent' and 'good practice' on the part of schools. This can result in unrealistic expectations, ill-thought-out initiatives and frustration at perceived parental apathy on the part of teachers. Talking to parents, on the other hand, often reveals considerable levels of concern about secondary education: many feel ill-informed, distanced and often frustrated by the lack of effective communication between them and the school.

What is clear is that the lack of debate about parental involvement at secondary level and the lack of sharing successful strategies has done little to improve the situation or to spread good practice. This chapter aims to examine and debate some of the often unconscious assumptions and key issues which seem to underpin this area of work, to attempt a redefinition of parental involvement which is more appropriate to the changed circumstances of secondary education and to outline some practical strategies for development.

The authors draw on many years of practical experience in schools in both Scotland and England. They have focused primarily on the relationships between parents and urban schools – where their main experience lies – although many of the points raised have wider application.

'They just don't care – they don't even bother to come to parents' evening'

This comment, which echoes in staffrooms throughout the country, reflects two related and common assumptions – firstly that parental involvement is primarily about parents' physical presence in schools and, more specifically, that whether a parent attends a parents' evening is a definitive indicator of their general interest in their child's education. Indeed assessment of parental interest is invariably related to their physical presence whether at a parents evening, behind a stall at a summer fair or by an immediate appearance following a summons to deal with a problem. This emphasis on the parent coming into school may be especially inappropriate at secondary level.

Experience of working directly with parents confirms that most parents do, in fact, care deeply about their child's education. It is in communicating that concern that the problem arises. Schools, by dictating very specifically how parents should show their interest sometimes create very difficult and threatening situations for them. For many parents the physical environment of a secondary school can be intimidating, carrying memories of powerlessness and failure from their own schooldays. Schools can appear full of adults, with their expertise and incomprehensible jargon, apparently waiting to make judgements on their child and implicitly on their parenting.

Furthermore, for adolescents school presents an important environment where they can experience a measure of independence from their parents. The increasing importance of peer authority may mean young people are highly sensitive to their peer's opinions of their parents. As a result parents may receive some very ambiguous messages from their offspring about the desirability of their presence in school.

Several strategies seem appropriate in response to this issue. Firstly, the relationship between parents and schools can be thought about more widely and creatively by offering a variety of ways of making contact which do not always depend on parents physically coming into school. This might include greater use of the telephone, meetings outside the school environment i.e. in a local library, leisure centre or centre frequented by the community, home visits, more effective two-way written communications, using tapes, videos or CD Roms or the use of mediators such as education welfare officers. Secondly, there is a need to think very carefully about the welcome and care parents receive when they do come into school. Are they greeted well? Do they know where to go? Is there somewhere comfortable and preferably private to wait? Are there refreshments and interpreters available if necessary? Is the school accessible? Are there toys available if they have young children? Given that parents may be nervous, their first experiences of the school need to be as positive, relaxing and familiar as possible.

'Parents can't really help their child when it comes to secondary education'

The second assumption often made is that by secondary level most parents have little to contribute in directly supporting their children's education. As children grow older the influence and help given by parents is a hidden factor, often only acknowledged when it is lacking. Little thought is given to the important but difficult role that a parent takes in trying to support their teenager with their work at home. Occasionally the hours some parents spend struggling with their child's homework will emerge. However, in many cases parents will not have the education or knowledge to help their children with specific subjects and it is important that schools and parents recognise and value the range of practical tasks that parents can undertake to support their children's work at home and at school: providing a good working environment, knowing about deadlines and time management, helping young people develop study skills, asking useful questions, knowing about sources of further help such as encyclopaedias and libraries, and building confidence through encouragement. Simply acknowledging or giving parents the confidence that they can make a difference without having to understand fully the curriculum seems to be the key. As Sallis (1989) says:

> It doesn't matter if people are poor, uneducated, non-English speaking, illiterate. The only thing which had made the, in the educational sense, inadequate parents was the belief that they were inadequate. The message that anything they did could make a measurable difference to their children' progress was enough to work the magic.

Work with teenagers also, however, requires subtler skills. It may involve acknowledging when too much pressure can be counter productive, and parents knowing when to let go and when they have to leave the decisions, however difficult this may be, to their child. The difficulties of negotiating with teenagers and tactfully supporting them in their work is an issue that causes many parents enormous anxiety and deserves greater opportunities for discussion and help – a point which will be returned to later in the chapter.

A project in Castlebrae Community High School, Edinburgh worked with a group of twelve Year 9 pupils, their parents and English department staff to explore whether specific action by parents to support their children in the home could impact positively on the children's performance in class. The selection criteria for the groups was underachievement but no serious behaviour problems. The project comprised five sessions. In the first two the parents reflected on their own experience of school and how that had shaped their attitudes towards school in the present. The third session was spent with the English department staff who explained in detail the course structure and content. The fourth and fifth sessions focused on looking at what parents could do which might help their children do better. As a result each parent drew up a checklist of simple practical action which they and the English staff agreed might make a difference. These were things which in many cases they already did without being aware of their value. This included asking their child about books they were reading, praising them when they made an effort, getting them to tell them a story and keeping distractions out of the way (e.g. turning the TV off).

Immediate evaluation of the initiative demonstrated at least some noticeable improvement in attitude and levels of motivation among all of the pupils involved. Further evaluation will be required to assess whether any of the improvement has been sustained over a longer period. Some unexpected benefits also seemed to accrue. Staff acknowledged that in some cases their views of parents had altered and consequently they now felt they related 'differently' to the students concerned. There was also sometimes a significant effect on the relationship between the parents and children – in one case a parent perceived the most significant benefit to be the improved communication with her son.

Apart from the Castlebrae project there are many other strategies for helping parents support their children at secondary level:

- Workshops and open days can provide opportunities for very practical experience and give more specific knowledge about the curriculum. They also create situations where children can demonstrate their skills and knowledge and talk to their parents about their work.
- Homework projects which specifically involve parents can work well at the lower end of secondary school although they need to be undertaken with sensitivity towards parents who might find it difficult to help or who may not have the time or energy.
- Clearer information about what children are learning and how parents can help them can be available through year booklets, brochures,

letters or newsletters. A Year 10 parents' group at one school asked for better information about GCSE coursework deadlines so that they could help chase up work.

- Homework can be a contentious issue and is often the focus for adolescent/parent conflict, but for some schools the development of homework policies, clearer information about homework and homework diaries have helped to clarify boundaries and expectations for pupils, staff and parents.

- Offering parents opportunities to return to education themselves can break a cycle of educational failure in a family. Parents are often open to such opportunities when children start secondary school and schools, if not able to provide opportunities themselves, can put them in touch with adult education or other relevant organisations. Parents returning to evening classes can be a powerful role model for their children as well as developing their own ability, interest and confidence in supporting their child.

'Some parents just aren't bothered – you can't reach them'

Another implicit assumption, as raised earlier, is that if parents don't conform to the school's requirements, they don't care about their child's education. Being a good parent in the school's eyes is, as Meighan (1986) points out, a tricky business:

> Parents vary in their reading of the schools definition of a good parent as well as their subsequent reactions. Some fail in collecting sufficient reliable information about the school and can easily fall into the trap of being seen as neglectful, others take too keen an interest to become interferers, others decide to be admiring spectators only to be seen as apathetic.

He goes on to argue that the 'good' parent does not need to be well informed or in agreement with the school's ideology, only to give the impression that this is the case. He describes how middle-class parents may well have more skills not only to help their child, but also to manage the correct impression for the teachers.

An implicit assumption which seems to be held by many schools is that all parents will respond uniformly and have similar resources, skills and experience. Very often communications are aimed at one particular group served by the school – and this is often the one closest to the teachers own experience – white and middle class. There have been some striking examples of schools being ill-informed about the parents and the communities they serve – a problem that becomes more complex when it involves a number of very disparate groups in relation to class or culture.

The need to know and understand the parents and the community the school serves is paramount. In particular, schools need to have mechanisms to listen to the views and needs of different groups of parents through surveys or open meetings, informal interviews at parents' evenings or home visiting. There are many ways to reach out to different parents:

- Some schools have found it useful to explore very varied family, community or religious structures through which to communicate. This might include notices in popular local shops or clubs or working through key local community figures such as religious leaders.
- Developing personal contact and relationships is always the most effective way to build bridges.
- Some schools have put on particular social events which might appeal to specific cultural or social groups served by the school.
- Building on strengths is also often important. Positive contact can be initiated when the parent feels they can offer something e.g. a useful contact for work experience, something for a summer fair, information for a project the children are doing, or when the school can offer something that parents need very directly e.g. bargains, practical advice.

Parents are as individual as a mixed-ability class and often want very different amounts and types of information, contact and involvement. Providing a range of opportunities and flexibility of structures may help to meet the needs of a wider group of parents.

'It's the parents who are to blame'

Handling a disruptive teenager in a class of 30 children can be a very frustrating job and teachers inevitably turn to parents to provide support and sanctions. When parents fail to provide this the impression is often that they are indifferent or uncooperative but it also seems very easy for teachers to forget what a difficult job it is to parent teenagers. Apparent indifference can cover feelings of powerlessness and inadequacy. Parents, as Coleman points out, have to cope with the worries associated with the teenage years in a context where there are are not only increasing pressures around issues such as drugs, but also a real ambiguity in society about parental roles and responsibilities. Teachers, sometimes unreasonably, expect unresourced, untrained, often unsupported parents to cope and are frustrated when they don't manage it. As Coleman (1994) points out, 'blaming parents for the shortcomings of their adolescents is not a helpful approach'.

He goes on to suggest that there is widespread ignorance about normal adolescent development and that parents desperately need information, support and even the opportunities to identify and develop the very different skills required to parent teenagers:

> The overwhelming majority of adults who care for teenagers are undertaking a difficult task with commitment. Some do it extremely well, some not so well. It is up to us as professionals to acknowledge that there are stresses and strains inherent in parenting or caring for teenagers – especially for the troubled ones – and that those engaged in this task need support.
>
> (Coleman, 1994)

If teachers start with the attitude that parents are doing their best and that everyone needs to work together to find solutions and compromises – it may be possible to avoid the trap of blame and recrimination. Individual parents can indeed easily become pathologised – labelled as 'the problem' and as inadequate. However, where parents can meet together, broader common issues and problems related to the situation can be identified and potential solutions shared.

Some schools have looked at providing opportunities for parents to share experiences and get support through year or tutor group meetings. Beresford describes the experience of:

> enabling parents to meet together to discover common ideas and concerns and to develop collective consciousness and solidarity. Through various year groups I have seen the relief of parents realising they are not the only ones facing a problem. In a fourth year parents' group recently an animated account by one parent of the problems of bringing up an awkward teenager and the shame associated with attending parents' evenings was greeted with relieved laughter, echoes of similar experiences and real support.
>
> (1992)

In Sweden, at the start of secondary education, many parents attend a series of meetings in class groups which introduce them to both the school and curriculum and also to some of the issues related to parenting teenagers. Many schools have also looked at providing better information for parents about adolescence and associated issues such as drugs or contacts with other organisations who might be able to help.

'Teenagers want their parents to be involved throughout their school life'

Adolescence undoubtedly complicates home–school relationships. As has already been stated, young people of secondary school age may feel very ambiguous about their parents' involvement in school. 'Pupils of secondary age ... may feel that schools are their world, not their parents', and it is essential that teachers and parents recognise this' (ILEA, 1988).

Watkins (1987) more strongly suggests that as the adolescent is negotiating release from the family the relationship between parents, home and school should be reduced – 'A progressive reduction of contact in the later years of secondary school would be exactly appropriate for the impending separation and also perhaps for the adolescent.' This may be appropriate to some extent but there also seems to be a danger of misinterpreting the apparent distancing or rejection by adolescents. As Coleman (1994) points out it isn't that adolescents don't need their parents but that their needs are expressed in a different way. Young people who find it difficult to ask directly for their parents' support may in fact be grateful for school maintaining communication with their parents. Young people still need their parents' encouragement and interest in education, but the ways in which parents express this may need to be more subtle.

Clearly, for instance, the concept of daytime parent volunteers in school may not be appropriate, although evening meetings where parents will not come into contact with their embarrassed children's peers are often more acceptable.

Studies by Harter (1990) on the development of self-concept and self-esteem show that teenagers are more influenced by the way their parents view and evaluate them than by any other factor. The negativity surrounding public images of adolescents is often reflected in relationships between parents and adolescents who become highly critical of each other. Schools easily feed into this cycle. One secondary school, on reviewing letters home discovered that 95 per cent of them were negative. Schools need to make sure that they provide opportunities to communicate positive achievements to parents.

Another issue which arises as the child grows older relates to who is in fact 'the client' – the young person or their parents. This is reflected in a number of practical issues – are records of achievement addressed to the pupil or the parent, at what stage do teachers involve parents if there are problems and indeed what information do schools pass on about, for instance, a child's drug taking or sexual activity?

This is part of a wider ambiguity in society about young people and responsibility reflected in legal cases on advice on contraception or demands for parents to pay the fines for teenage crime. Society seems to give mixed, perhaps impossible, messages to parents (and sometimes schools) about their roles and responsibilities in relation to their teenage children.

It is often in parents' evenings where the lack of clarity about this issue is epitomised. Do young people attend parents evenings with their parents? If their parents don't attend can they attend on their own? If they do come, how does the teacher handle what is often a very complex three-way situation engaging not just the establishment of the relationship between the teacher and parent, but also the the relationship between the teacher and child and the parent and child. Does the teacher address comments to the child or the parent? How do they draw all parties in or respond if the relationship between the parents and child is uncomfortable? It is a highly skilled engagement for which teachers have little or no preparation but which can have a profound effect on the relationship between child and parent.

Young people can also play a vital role in working alongside parents. Evenings on educational issues can include young people as well as parents. School councils or pupils' committees can work together with Parent Teacher Associations to organise events or fundraising, and family evenings, particularly at the lower end of secondary school, can provide opportunities for parents and children to learn new skills related to art, music or information technology.

It is interesting that in the United States some schools see part of their role as helping parents let go of their children and they run special workshops for parents. Certainly it seems clear that home–school relationships need to be reviewed and adjusted as a young person grows older and naturally takes on more responsibility for their own education. Young people as well as their parents need to be consulted, where appropriate, about decisions which affect them.

Young people themselves are crucial carriers of information to parents and often undertake their own vetting of what they regard as necessary or useful for parents to see. To take time to explain and discuss with young people their parents' involvement instead of bypassing them or using them as rather unreliable messengers can be very beneficial.

'Just send it out to them – it doesn't really matter how'

Communication with the home is clearly crucial if parents are to become informed, but schools should be judicious in the timing, quantity and quality of the approaches which they make to parents. It is important to resist the temptation to bombard parents indiscriminately with information. The less a school discriminates between all of the potential communications it could have with the home the less likely it is that parents will be in a position to respond appropriately. In addition to the problem of parents being unable to distinguish between what is and isn't important as a result of the junk mail approach, its psychological impact on parents should be considered. This runs something along the lines of 'when you've said "no" once it comes easier the second time and even easier after that'. By telling parents everything or inviting parents to every event possible the school runs the risk of killing any interest stone dead.

Equally, it is important to research what information parents *do* want and need through surveys, discussions at parents associations or parents' groups or informal interviews at parents' evenings. There may, in some schools, be a real lack of information or potentially a lack of access to further information for parents who do want to know more. One strategy is to find out which parents might be interested in getting more involved in particular activities or want to know more and telephone or send out extra information to them.

If schools decide to be more selective in choosing when and how to make their approaches to parents, what criteria should they use? An important and useful concept is that of key moments. At the point of transition to secondary schools the sense of a new beginning can lead to a genuine interest in reactivating the relationship with school. In addition as the point of transition approaches and in the weeks after the school session commences parents often experience intense anxiety as they are concerned about how well their child will cope with the new demands of secondary school. This reawakened interest in school provides an opportunity to change previous patterns of involvement with school and to develop a more active relationship which has the potential to be sustained long after the point of transition has passed.

Other key occasions which merit more in-depth communication might include subject choices, preparation for examinations, and transition to the world of work or further education. However, in every case the onus is on the school to ensure that when it communicates with parents at these times it is clear what is expected of them. Wherever possible, suggestions should be made by the school which relate to practical things that parents can do to help their child. All too often parents are left to make sense of large amounts of complex information without adequate briefing on the background or any suggestions as to what they should do with it. Ensuring information is well-presented, jargon-free, translated where necessary and really accessible to the lay reader is also clearly crucial. One of the best ways to check information is through the comments of a small group of representative parents.

A further consideration when reviewing home–school communications relates to the different perspectives of the two sides of the relationship. The parent is primarily concerned with individualised, detailed information about their child. While the school has to view its student population as a whole and across the full range of its departments' differing experiences of each child. In order to develop a positive relationship with such a multifaceted organisation as a school the parent has to be confident that within the organisation there is a common understanding of their child and that the teachers and departments are able to communicate effectively with each other. Unfortunately the school is not always able to present the coordinated front it would like to and it is not unheard of for departmental concerns about any one child to be conveyed to the parent by separate departments without reference to one another. The resultant confusion, and the potentially contradictory messages which are sent to the parent, undermine confidence in school systems and are unlikely to generate a greater willingness on the part of the parent to collaborate with the school in the future. Central to any strategy for effective communications with parents has to be a commitment from within the school to manage and maintain a proper overview of all contacts with the home and to ensure efficient channels of communication and cooperation exist across all of the school's departments.

Schools therefore need to examine their communications carefully and check out whether:

- their timing is appropriate;
- the response expected is clear;
- there is an effective overview;
- information is well presented and accessible;
- the school has strategies for checking out what parents do want and need.

'Teachers are well prepared for their work with parents'

From issues raised above it can be seen that a wide range of skills are required for developing home–school relations which are very different from the skills of managing children in a classroom situation. The skills of listening to parents, planning, organising and facilitating groups, communicating appropriately with adults, negotiating, counselling and managing volunteers are rarely covered in initial teacher training. Teachers, therefore, are ill-prepared for this work and often do not recognise the skills needed. The Metropolitan Life Survey (1987) found that many teachers were reluctant even to approach parents. Not surprisingly, many teachers feel nervous and unskilled and this can lead to avoidance of this type of work or a situation where they do not adapt their behaviour to adults and can appear patronising, didactic or insensitive to parents' own experience and needs. Secondary school teachers being more subject based are often even less likely to feel confident in this role. Schools need to consider work with parents as a topic for INSET and teacher-training courses need to look carefully at how they are preparing teachers for this work. If teachers could broaden their perception of their role, then their skills work with parents would have a far greater chance of being effective.

'The aim is to get complete agreement – then there should be no conflict between home and school'

As a complex organisation inevitably a school has a multiplicity of relationships with each of its parents. Through policies and common practices the school attempts to define a relationship with the parent population as a whole and sets out a framework within which all individual interactions with parents occur. If procedures are clear and well communicated, the culture is positive and good relationships have been developed conflict will undoubtedly be lessened. But to attempt to obliterate conflict completely is unrealistic and maybe unhealthy. Some conflict is inevitable. By their nature parents and schools have a different orientation – one towards their individual child and the other towards the whole establishment – and adolescence is necessarily a time of friction.

The skill is in the creative management of conflict rather than its avoidance and in developing a productive and fruitful relationship where both sides are more informed and each has greater sensitivity to the needs and circumstances of the other.

Conclusion

What we have attempted to argue in this chapter is that parental involvement at secondary level should not primarily be focused on the physical presence of parents in schools but on using a wide range of strategies to develop accessible two-way communication and to recognise, encourage and support parents in feeling that they can make a difference to their child's progress. Schools need to understand and respect the very varied needs and strengths of the parents and communities they serve and the particular stresses that the parents of teenagers face. It is also vital to recognise the important role of the young person themselves within the home–school relationship and allow this relationship to change appropriately, although not necessarily to lessen, as the young person becomes increasingly independent. Furthermore, schools themselves can be enriched by tapping into the resources, experiences and skills that parents can offer and can benefit from listening to the views and ideas of parents. Developing relationships with parents at secondary level is a difficult but crucial task.

References

Beresford, E. (1992) 'The Politics of Parental Involvement' in Allen, G. and Martin, I. *Education and Community*. London: Cassell.

Coleman, J. (1994) *The Parenting of Teenagers*. A talk given at a National Children's Bureau conference 'Confident Parents, Confident Children', London, 27 September.

Harter, S. (1990) 'Self and Identity Development', in Feldman, S. and Elliott, G. (eds) *At the Threshold*. London: Routledge.

ILEA (1988) *Parental Involvement in Secondary Schools*. ILEA Learning Resources Branch.

Meighan, R. (1986) *A Sociology of Educating*. London: Cassell.

Metropolitan Life Insurance Company (1987) 'The Metropolitan Life Survey of the American Teacher 1987: strengthening the links between home and school', *Report on Educational Research*, 19 (18): 3–4.

Sallis, J. (1989) *Schools, Parents and Governors: a new approach to accountability*. London: Routledge.

Watkins, C. (1987) 'Parental Involvement in the Upper School', *Pastoral Care in Education*, 5 (2), Jan: 77–85.

14 Home to school is a long way: facing up to the issues of developing home–school alliances in rural areas

Tanny Stobart

The hour and a half it takes to walk three miles when accompanied by a nine-year-old with a 'yo yo' walking style gives plenty of time for reflection, for example, some ungrateful thoughts about people who spend the weekend dismantling the Ford Capri which is the School Transport, and some anxious ones about whether it will be fixed by next week.

When we lived in London school was close, another was near and to some extent we had a choice about which to go to. If it was raining we could walk to a neighbour whose children went to the same school, and share shepherding them backwards and forwards. You would think there would be a local bus here, but the only one that comes up our way is on Tuesdays and Saturdays.

If you live further away from school they provide school transport which is good – but you miss talking to other parents. You learn a lot about what happens in school and about bringing up kids standing at the school gate. If I can keep the 'yo yo' moving we will get to school in time and perhaps I will meet somebody who can give me a lift back … or will I be walking five hours a day?

What is rural?

The Office of Population Censuses and Surveys (OPCS) offer several definitions. Using a 'dwellings' approach they define an urban area as a predominantly built-up area covering four or more census enumeration districts. This approach includes most small towns/large villages with 1,000 or more inhabitants. Everywhere else is rural. Then after the 1981 census the OPCS categorised each enumeration district as urban or non-urban (rural) on the basis of the percentage of the population living in urban areas. They put all the electoral wards on a scale – 'wholly urban–completely rural'. They then ranked the 403 districts in England and Wales in terms of the proportion of the population living in predominantly rural mixed or urban wards.

Various other organisations and people have developed systems and definitions of rurality. They may use different characteristics and indicators and different classifications emerge. Group classification may include:

- rural with a transient population;
- remote rural;
- less remote but still mainly rural;
- more rural than urban but with industry.

Many organisations apply area or settlement definitions to bring rural areas into focus and then use local networks and research to identify needs. For example the Rural Development Commission (RDC) is a national government agency which promotes economical and social development in rural England. It defines rural committees as 'those with up to 10,000 inhabitants' and offers business advice and help with community development. Much of the RDC funding is targeted on 27 Rural Development Areas (RDAs).

It is not unusual for people and organisations to make distinctions between rural and urban areas and there is no single definition. Some emphasise the physical and environmental differences, others the social and economic.

Recent economic and social changes affecting rural families

It is clear that recent economic, demographic and social changes across Europe are having a significant effect on many rural families today.

In agriculture increased productivity has almost doubled the volume of output and led to a significant decline in employment. Over the past few years the subsidies which farmers have enjoyed have been steadily eroded and in many areas this has led to an increase in non-agricultural activities at farm households – including the production of cheese, wine and yoghurts and the development of tourist activities like bed and breakfast, activity holidays and other recreational services. The difficulties facing the fishing industry are also well documented (Cohen, 1995: 12).

In some places jobs lost in agriculture may result in redistribution of the rural population and the migration to towns or cities. However, some rural areas, usually those within easy reach of cities, have seen an increase in population where people are moving from the city to the countryside either to follow employment, cheaper housing or an improved quality of life. Alongside these economic changes is the increased level of participation of women in the labour market. This has been particularly associated with the development of the service sector. 'In rural areas the service sector now employs over 65 per cent of the female workforce and in some rural regions, for example in The Netherlands and the UK, over 80 per cent' (Cohen, 1995: 14).

Recent research involving families with young children in rural Devon by Halliday at Exeter University also confirmed similar characteristics within the research sample interviewed:

> Overall, nearly one third are employed in personal services such as catering, cleaning, hairdressing and caring (often in residential homes) this is followed in frequency by clerical work and retail/farming in equal third place. Together these four sectors account for over two thirds of the employment.
>
> (Halliday, 1995: 31)

There is not only an increase in the number of women entering the labour market, but also as Bronwen Cohen describes:

> The greater visibility of women within the labour market associated with shift from 'informal' work in the form of assisting a spouse in family enterprise such as farming or fishing to obtaining jobs within the formal labour market.
>
> (Cohen, 1995: 14)

This also correlates with the Halliday research of working mothers in the sample:

> It is notable that only just one half are employees, one quarter are self employed and one fifth work in the family business (often in an unpaid capacity) the majority (65 per cent) work outside the home and have permanent (91 per cent) as opposed to seasonal or temporary jobs. Few work shifts.
>
> (Halliday, 1995: 31)

Other significant changes in rural life include limited local services and poor public transport. This has worsened since deregulation; some villages are not served at all and many villages now have as few as one bus a week to the nearby town. Many more people work from home; most commuters depend on cars. This is also borne out in the Halliday research:

> 15 per cent of households in the study area lacked a car while, at the other end of the spectrum over one third of households had two or more cars. These high levels of car ownership are typical of rural areas where poor or non existent public transport means private transport is a necessity.
>
> (Halliday, 1995: 17)

There is also a high percentage of house-owner occupiers in rural communities. 'Just over three quarters of households in the study area own their home either outright or with a mortgage' (Halliday, 1995: 18). Although owning your own home and car might be taken as indicators of affluence, the reality is that poverty for rural families is a hidden factor. Rural wages are significantly lower than the national average.

Glossy images of the countryside mask a whole range of deprivation and disadvantage – poverty, repressive attitudes, lack of access to opportunities, alienation of non-conformers from public life, intolerance of 'deviant' behaviour. Official statistics usually under record the full extent of social and economic problems. People in housing need, for example, do not register on the council house waiting list if they know that there is no available housing in their village.

(Francis and Henderson, 1994: 3–4)

But is rural deprivation different from its urban counterpart? Probably the main difference is that deprivation in the country exists in isolated pockets. It is difficult to identify a household which is experiencing great poverty in a village which is mainly affluent.

Many villages harbour enormous contrasts between wealth and poverty, different cultures and ways of life. The collection of pretty well-maintained cottages and houses are homes to people living in abject poverty as well as to some of the wealthiest people in the country.

(Francis and Henderson, 1994: 8)

It is also statistically difficult to identify rural deprivation. For example: the high costs for a family living in the country to access services, which are taken for granted in a town, are not known. Virtually all the statistics which are used in cities fail to take account of these special factors which are a feature of country life. This may be simply due to the dearth of indicators derived from census material. For example, the census collects information about car ownership but not about the distance from the health centre or the local school.

Below, fourteen indicators are listed, which may be used to pinpoint rural deprivation:

1 lack of local services and facilities including medical services, public telephones, post offices, banks, job centres and social security offices;

2 higher living costs – more expensive petrol, higher prices for foodstuffs at village shops;

3 lack of low-cost housing. Many rural areas also have poor quality housing with poor amenities;

4 lack of public transport. Greater reliance on own transport with an increased cost of living;

5 greater distances from sources of information including advice and counselling. Telephone costs increase with greater distances;

6 lack of local job opportunities, especially for women without their own transport;

7 part-time and seasonal employment. Lower rates of pay;

8 lack of local sports and leisure facilities;

9 lack of adult education and vocational training opportunities. Greater travel costs incurred when accessing classes;

10 limited services for different groups within the community such as the elderly, people with disability, pre-school children, women and the long-term unemployed;

11 lack of political influence because of a smaller voting public;

12 traditionally held family views can lead to stigmatising of certain groups, the single parent families, unemployed people;

13 limited control over local resources highlighted by land ownership patterns and the distance from the seat of local government;

14 lack of anonymity at local services such as the doctors.

Many of these indicators are interdependent and although some of these problems could be addressed by local networks, these, too, are often underdeveloped.

Home to school is a long way

Against this backdrop, developing partnerships between home and school in the countryside has been patchy and in some places non-existent. For many rural parents saying goodbye to their children at the end of a lane where the school bus stops is the daily routine. The regular opportunity for these rural parents to meet teachers to find out about their children's progress or talk to other parents at the school gate is not an option. The result is that the possibilities of building family support networks, receiving helpful advice and developing home–school alliances are all substantially reduced.

> Low levels of awareness are often associated with a shortage or absence of information over what is possible and what can be achieved. Access to information may be affected by geographical isolation and the costs of providing information services. In some areas this is affected by adult literacy.
> (Cohen, 1995: 62)

As new people move into rural communities and local people move out, those who remain are increasingly exposed to outside influences by education, television, radio and so on. This can have a significant affect on some indigenous members of the community and those who are less confident.

Schools may encourage parents to come and listen to the children reading, but this is not much good if there is a problem with literacy which a parent may not wish to admit to, preferring to avoid any possibility of village gossip. It can be difficult to be anonymous in a small community.

It could also be argued that the promotion of home–school links is deculturalising families and their outlook on school. There is a contradiction between government policy which espouses Local Management of Schools (LMS) while at the same time using home–school links to tighten its grip on the way families behave, i.e. good parenting = school involvement, bad parenting = no involvement. In the country where at parish and local authority level the power tends to lie with long-standing families, wealthier residents and the key professionals like teachers, the needs of rural families and the particular problems of isolation, transport and extended working hours which they face are not recognised. In the recent Halliday research the majority (68 per cent) of mothers interviewed worked. All of them had children under five and some also had school-aged children. At least two-fifths of them had other regular demands on their time including helping at their children's school.

> The largest group worked between 16 and 30 hours per week and one fifth worked full-time. Only one fifth had not worked since they had a family. The second adult within the family was likely to be in full-time employment and work long hours (16 per cent worked in agriculture).
>
> (Halliday, 1995: 31)

During this research it was found that over three-fifths had left the home by 8.00 am and more than one-fifth had left by 7.00 am. At the other end of the day more than half returned by 6.00 pm with some 16 per cent returning after 8.00 pm. Departures started at 3.45 am and returns continued until 11.00 pm.

Although there can be little doubt that the village school, usually the primary school, has a vital role to play in rural life, the extent and the quality of its involvement will depend largely on the attitudes and commitment of its one or two members of staff. Taking into account the recent changes for teachers who are working hard to introduce the National Curriculum, there may be an understandable reluctance to introduce parent-involvement initiatives. And of course parents in rural areas do not have the advantage of a choice of school unless they are prepared to travel significant distances when home to school is already a long way.

Developing new approaches

'Low expectations, slow adjustment to change, a class and a power struggle where "everyone knows their place", and a limited experience of collective action, are all commonplace in rural communities' (Francis and Henderson, 1994: 4). The result is that even though rural parents may be aware of the value of home–school alliances, their involvement with schools is usually for a 'service' purpose like raising money at the school fete or helping out at a school disco. The opportunities for rural parents in the UK to involve themselves in their children's learning are still very patchy.

The development of rural family and parent education initiatives has usually been as a direct result of intervention by a community or family worker or by the introduction of a support network. However, the costs attached to the developing, organising and delivering a rural programme tends to be much higher than a similar urban initiative. Development workers can also find that there is a reluctance to change and things can take much longer to happen, so that the costs escalate.

However, there are now numerous examples across the country where home–school partnerships have been established (Pugh *et al.*, 1994: 182–8). In Devon, much of which could be described as rural, the experience of developing family education initiatives over the last ten years has been informed by a particular code of practice based on a set of values. The practice is about sharing and accessing information, resources and opportunities in a supportive and encouraging way. It recognises that the right advice or information may be all people need to take action themselves.

The values are based on the belief that people have the ability and the right to make an active and positive contribution to their own and their families learning, to the community and to the wider world.

However, if you live in a tiny rural Devon village with small children and do not drive or have ready access to the family car, taking advantage of a family education project, even if a few miles away, is difficult! Since deregulation, many villages do not have a daily bus service and the only buses which run may not fit in with other things like feeding the baby and meeting the school bus.

Recognising that people like to stay in their villages to develop their own activities and networks, the Crediton Neighbourhood Family Centre was established as a self-help initiative to meet the particular needs of local families. The plan was to send workers to the villages with information and toys to run family learning sessions.

> Letters were sent out to see who was interested and as many as twelve villages said that they would like a visit from a mobile toy library and family workshop. The trailer, toys and equipment were purchased as a result of local fund-raising and the help of the Villages in Action scheme. Now eight villages are visited once per month. Local parents are involved in the planning and the running of activities.
>
> This venture is jointly supported by the statutory agencies and its success is spreading.
>
> (Stobart *et al.*, 1994: 40)

Family education in Devon is part of the Devon County Council's Community Education Service. The Family Education Resources Network Committee (known as County FERN) works in close collaboration with the County Council and is able to advise on policy issues. County FERN has four sub-committees known as Area FERNs. Their membership includes project workers, participants and interested people in north, south, east and west Devon.

The function of an Area FERN is to act as a forum for the airing and sharing of ideas and to support training activities. Networking is central to the development of family education in Devon and is particularly important to the development of parent school partnerships.

> Family Reading Matters is the name of a small group of parents whose children attend a rural primary school and who have come together to look at ways of helping their children to read.
>
> Colourful picture cards, beautiful drawings of fish, weeds, shells and rocks on three laminated cards which, clipped together, form the sides of a pond. A bag of letters and three fishing rods each fitted with a tiny magnet ... and it's a game! Fish for a letter, pull it out and decide which picture to put it on. Then fish for another. This is just one of the many reading games designed and made by parents to help them help their children improve their reading at home.
>
> (Stobart *et al.*, 1994: 14)

This project started with a small group of parents and a parent education worker who decided to find out from other parents if they were interested in helping their children to read. They wrote and circulated a questionnaire. The results revealed an overwhelming commitment by parents to support their children in their first stages of reading. The parents then gathered information from teachers, this was collated and discussed. The production of materials to help parents help their children then followed. They also produced a video which provided examples of reading techniques which parents can take home to look at and study in their own time.

> Over nine months for one hour per week the Family Reading Matters parents of children at Bluecoats Infant School in Torrington have produced an impressive amount of work. The vitality of the project comes from the awareness and support of staff and from the commitment of parents who can see the benefit to their children.
>
> (Stobart *et al.*, 1994: 15)

This work is only one example of the numerous rural family education projects going on in the UK, in Europe and in the States (Pugh *et al.*, 1994: 182–8). The key to this learning is recognised in a recent policy discussion paper produced by NIACE:

The central question is the extent to which family members are the key decision makers over the content, direction and form of learning. Where they are imposed on families they are usually ineffective, often inappropriate and sometimes counter productive. This has to be understood in terms of the context and the historical evolution of family learning.

(Alexander and Clyne, 1995: 7)

The recent comprehensive publication *Confident Parents, Confident Children* also recognised that:

Opportunities for parents' involvement in their children's schools, whether in a general way or as their children's educators or in extending their own development and learning, appear to have increased in some localities and to have had positive outcomes for both parents and children.

(Pugh *et al.*, 1994: 218)

It also recognised that:

Although all parents have a need for a 'bare level' of support there are some for whom this needs to be adapted to their particular needs, and we have been able to cite good examples of work with families with disabled children, with disabled parents, with lone parents, teenage parents, parents in custody, black and minority ethnic families and with fathers.

(Pugh *et al.*, 1994: 218)

However, what is not discussed by either of these recent important studies are the particular needs of people living in very rural areas. This cannot be because of the size of the issue. Almost 25 per cent of people in the UK live in rural areas. Today the issues that affect parents in the urban areas are equally important to those living rurally. For the first time since the industrial revolution rural communities are perceived as having the opportunity to benefit from technological change on an equal footing with their urban counterparts. There is a general trend towards the decentralisation of economic activity. Technologies above all else give an opportunity for decentralisation whether in the form of small units linked by telecommunication or remote access to information and professional services.

It is, however, recognised that there are additional complexities associated with setting up and maintaining parent education provision in rural areas. To move from an inadequate and under-funded service to high quality provision in every rural hamlet would be difficult. In this climate of change there is a need to generate and maintain a cooperative and collaborative approach to the support for provision.

The following quote is part of a submission from Devon County Council and County FERN to the All Parliamentary Group on Parenting in 1994:

'All children irrespective of where they are born or brought up should have equal access to good quality services' (European Commission 1990). The reality for parents and children in rural areas is that there is often very little choice and very limited access to services for families. There is now an increased recognition of the relationship of childcare and family education to other aspects of rural development, economic and social growth.

It is recommended that ministers in Central Government and local councillors should recognise the importance of family education and children's services to ensure provision and opportunities for all families. A lead department should be established within each local authority, allocated funding to respond to the needs of all families especially those in rural areas. When considering this recommendation it is important that Her Majesty's Government recognises and values the major role currently played by voluntary organisations in the delivery of these services. It is also therefore recommended that, alongside the lead department, a strong partnership and communication channels be established between local communities, local groups, the local authority and regional and national networks.

(All Party Parliamentary Group on Parenting Report 1994: 111)

The reality is that most policies tend to be urban-led. Rural areas require a national family policy which recognises the diverse range of functions which are needed to support families bringing up their children.

Developing home–school alliances in rural areas will depend upon a greater understanding of the very real issues that face families. For many, the difficulties facing Sue, outlined below, are not uncommon.

Sue is a single parent. She has four children, an eighteen-year-old who has just left home, a seven-year-old boy and three-year-old twin girls. One of the girls is a severe asthmatic who Sue treats at home with a nebuliser.

Sue originally came from Liverpool and has no family support locally. Her car 'died' about three months ago and she now has no transport of her own. She lives up a hill, two miles from a small village. What facilities there are in the area are located in the centre of the village and they include a school, a playgroup, a church and a village hall. The nearest recreation ground and play area is about a mile from the village in the opposite direction from Sue's house. There is a small sub post office which sells newspapers, magazines, sweets, canned drinks, Lyons cakes and bread. There are no other shops for fruit and vegetables, butchers, clothes or medicines. There is a Tesco Shoppers bus once a week which leaves the centre of the village at 11.00 am and returns at 3.00 pm, but does not go up the hill past Sue's home. Sue catches the bus once a fortnight (which coincides with the arrival of the Giro) and takes a taxi back with the shopping and the twins. There is a PTA at the school, this term they are holding a dinner dance, the tickets are £7.50 each and Sue cannot afford to buy one.

To be responsive to the needs of rural families like Sue's needs careful consideration from a range of perspectives. For example, the staff of one village school near Ilfracombe in very rural part of North Devon knew that there were a number of isolated parents with young children and no transport. There was no local playgroup and no space within the school for a group of parents and young children to meet during the day. Then as part of the school's refurbishment programme the outside toilet block was condemned and new ones installed in school. With a tremendous amount of support from parents and staff, lots of fundraising and 'do-it-yourself' expertise, the block has been transformed into a small community room. It is used every day and is often full to capacity with 6–8 families. There is a varied programme including a family workshop, a playgroup and a twins group. The family workshop leader works closely with the health visitor and will visit new families at home. They can help sort out problems like transport and shopping. They can also encourage and support parents to meet other parents, and develop a local programme to meet their needs. One family workshop leader explained: 'It works really well because we all want it to work, helpers, parents and teachers. What happens is the community room depends on what parents want and what the children are learning about in school.'

Although understanding starts with parents and teachers themselves, it will be important for those people who have a direct interest in the well being of families, including parent education workers, social workers, advisers, officers and politicians, to become more aware of these issues and find ways not only to support future work, but also future policies which take rurality seriously.

The recent establishment of the National Parenting Education and Support Forum brings together those concerned with or working in the field of education and support for parents. Hopefully it will promote and maintain a high profile for parent education, support and press for effective policies and practice to promote home–school alliances at both local and national level with the aims of serving the best interests of all including rural children and their families.

References

Alexander, T. and Clyne, P. (1995) *Riches Beyond Price – Making the Most of Family Learning.* 21 De Montfort Street, Leicester LE1 7GE: NIACE.

Cohen, B. (1995) *Childcare Services for Rural Families.* European Commission Network on Childcare and other measures to reconcile Employment and Family Responsibilities. Bronwen Cohen, Children in Scotland, Princes House, 5 Shandwick Place, Edinburgh EH2 4RG.

Francis, D. and Henderson, P. (1994) *Community Development and Rural Issues.* 60 Highbury Grove, London N5 2AG: Community Development Foundation Publications.

Halliday, J. (1995) *Children's Services and Care in Rural Devon*. Research Paper, University of Exeter, Amory Buildings, Rennes Drive, Exeter EX4 4RJ.

Parenting Education and Support Forum, Hetty Einzig, National Children's Bureau, 8 Wakley Street, London EC1V 7QE.

Pugh, G., De Ath, E. and Smith, C. (1994) *Confident Parents, Confident Children. Policy and practice in parent education and support*. London National Children's Bureau, 8 Wakley Street, London EX1V 7QE.

Report of the All Party Parliamentary Group on Parenting and International Year of the Family UK Parliamentary Hearings (1994) from The House of Commons, Westminster, London.

Stobart, T., Lake, L., Price, H., Brewer, P. and Hickling, G. (1994) *A Devon Approach to Family Education*. CCEU, Crossmead, Barley Lane, Exeter EX4 1TF: Devon County Council.

Index

Access schemes 80
accountability 1, 7
  developing power model 9, 11–13
  former power model 9–10
  governing bodies 8
  local education authorities (LEAs) 7–8
  parents 8–9
  schools 8, 11
  transitionary phase 9, 10
achievement,
  and ethnicity 62–3
  influence of home–school work 6
  in Newham 83, 86
  and poverty 91–2
  pupil achievement agenda 64–5
  role of parents 1, 15, 19–20, 83–93
adolescents,
  development 144–5
  support groups for parents 145
  see also secondary schools
adult education 64, 74, 77, 80–1
  secondary schools and 143
adult education tutors 44–5
advice and information centres 20–1, 128–37
Advisory Centre for Education (ACE) 128,
  129–30, 136
Aesop's Fables 41
Alexander, T., Bastiani, J. and
  Beresford, E. 68
Alexander, T. and Clyne, P. 160
All Party Parliamentary Group on Parenting
  Report 161
Allen, G., Bastiani, J., Martin, I. and Richards, K.
  85
assessment process, and
  Bangladeshi families 129
Atkin, J., Bastiani, J. and Goode, J. 54
attitudes to home–school work 1–2, 4
Audit Commission, report on child support
  services 17

Ball, C. 92
Bangladeshi families 120
  language problems 128
  relationship with schools 128–9
Barber, M. 91
Bastiani, J. 3, 29, 47, 61, 63, 95
Bastiani, J. and Doyle, N. 2, 48–9, 58
Bawa, B. 90
Begum, Syeda 39–40, 44
behaviour of pupils 64, 66
Bengali families 39–45
Beresford, E. 145
Bilingual Development Service and
  Consultancy, Liverpool 71

Blatch, Baroness 59
Bloom, B.S. 15
Bluecoats Infant School, Torrington 159
Boltery, M. 47, 49–50
Boy Who Cried Wolf, The 42
British Standards Institute 80

Castlebrae Community High School, Edinburgh
  142
catchment areas 3
Centre for Language in Primary Education 43
child abuse 16
Child Protection Register 16
Children Act (1989) 25, 48
City Challenge 59, 63, 83
  Action for Achievement Project 88–91
Clark, Reginald 21–2
class, and interaction with school 20
class size 91
Cohen, B. 153–4
Coleman, J. 144–5, 146
communication,
  between parents and adolescents 142
  between teachers and parents 1–2, 19, 24, 87,
    109, 140–1, 143–5, 147–9
  in effective families 22
  of home–school work 62
  surveys of pupils 54–5
community,
  effects of partnership on 74–5
  schools as focus for 24–6, 162
Community Coalition Project, Cleveland 63
Community Development Project (CDP) 99
community education centres 23
Community Education Strategy, Newham 85
community schools 18
confidence,
  in adolescents 146
  effects of partnership on 74–5
  of parents of secondary school pupils 141–2,
    144–5
  of parents with SEN children 137
  in rural areas 156
conflict between home and school 150
'creative' schools 120
Crediton Neighbourhood Family Centre, Devon
  158–9
crime, and family background 15, 18

David, M. 29
David, M. *et al.* 29
Davis, J. 103
Dearing Report 11
decision–making, by parents 129
Devon, family education 158–9, 160–1, 162

DfE,
  Basic Skills Unit 64, 80
  Choice and Diversity 48
differentiation, in home–school thinking and practice 3
Disability Living Allowance 136
divorce 16

early years networks 25
Education Act (1986) 49
Education Reform Act (1988) 48, 128
Education Reform Act (1990) 72, 75–6
education welfare officers 141
educational psychologists 129
effective schools,
  characteristics 4
embedding good practice 65–7
employment,
  allowing for time with children 23
  changing patterns 51
  and models of mothering 31
  and parental involvement 33–6
  in rural areas 153–4, 157
empowerment 47–56, 83, 87, 92–3
equal opportunities, in Newham 84, 85, 91
ethnicity,
  and achievement 62–3
  diversity in Newham 84
European Commission, on education in rural areas 160–1
evaluation 118
examination results, publication of 1
expectations,
  in effective families 22
  Home School Employment Partnership (HSEP), Paisley 97–8
  of mothers' role 30–1
  raising of 89–90
  in rural areas 157–8

family,
  changes in structure 2, 16, 51
  and crime 15, 18
  effective 19–23
  as foundation of learning 15, 19–20
  and inequality 16
  influence on achievement 15
  learning activities 22, 23
  relationships with school 2
  see also parents
family centres 137
family learning sessions 61
family literacy programmes 3, 64, 80, 81
Family Policy Council, Washington, USA 25
family services, co-ordination of 25–6
feminist analysis of home–school relations 30–1
Ferguslie Park, Paisley, Home School Employment Partnership (HSEP) 60, 95–104

Francis, D. and Henderson, P. 154–5, 157
Fullan, M. 99, 100
funding,
  of local education authorities (LEAs) 7
  for work with parents 13
Funding Agency for Schools (FAS) 7

Galloway, D. 128, 129, 131
gender discrimination, and parents' involvement in schools 28–37
governing bodies,
  accessibility 13
  accountability 8
  parents on 10, 66
  pupil involvement 49–50
  relationships with headteachers 10
  role of 1
  training courses 8
grant-maintained schools 7, 8
Grants for Education Support and Training (GEST) 63, 65, 131
Greenhill Community School, Oldham 54–5
Griffiths, S. 84
groupwork 24

Halliday, J. 154, 157
Hancock, R. 19, 118, 119, 131
Hancock, R. and Gale, S. 126
Hancock, R., Smith, P., Sheath, G. and Beetlestone, F. 118
Hannon, F.L., Weinberger, J. and Nutbrown, C. 19
Harbinger Video Project 118–26
  school profile 119–20
Harter, S. 146
Head Start 106
headteachers,
  accountability 8
  and parental involvement 34, 35–6
  relationships with governing bodies 10
health and social services 16–17, 25
Hegarty, Seamus 86
hidden agenda of parents' involvement 36–7, 62
home, as learning environment 106
Home School Employment Partnership (HSEP), Paisley 60, 95–104
  expectations 97–8
  influencing long-term change 98–102
  monitoring and evaluation 103–4
home visiting 20–1, 61, 66, 68, 101–2, 103, 134–5
home-learning schemes 17
homework,
  communication with parents 143
  projects 142
  see also IMPACT project; reading with children
Hoyle, E. 120

immigrant families 18
Bangladeshi 120, 128–9
Bengali 39–45
language problems 39, 128
and parental involvement 39–45
and Section 11 schemes 62–3
IMPACT project 17, 52, 64, 106
and assessment 114
background 106–7
benefits 113–14, 116
National Network 106–7
in practice 107–9
and quality of teaching 113–14
response rate 112–13
Shared Writing Project 107, 109–10, 114–15
theory of 110–11
use of diary 108–9, 113
and 'visibility' 114
in–service training (INSET) 5, 62, 65, 68, 77
'third–person' 114
inequality, and parental involvement 34, 35
information, parents' entitlement to 1
information technology 19
and rural areas 160
Inner City Partnership Initiative, *Policy of the Inner Cities* 70
Inner London Education Authority (ILEA) 128, 145
inspection of schools 1, 5, 58;
see also OFSTED

Jenner, Helen, and Harbinger Video Project 120, 123, 124
Johnson, D. and Ransom, E. 52–3
Jones, G., Bastiani, J., Chapman, C. and Bell, G. 47, 54

Labour Party, *Diversity and Excellence* 10, 11, 13
Lareau, A. 31
learning activities, in effective families 22, 23
learning society, future of 23–4
literacy,
family influence on 20
family literacy programmes 3, 64, 80, 81
methods used 42
parents' centres and 134, 135
reading schemes 42
see also reading with children
Liverpool City Council,
Learning to Regenerate 82
Policy for Community Education 73
Liverpool Parent School Partnership (PSP) *see* Parent School Partnership (PSP), Liverpool
local education authorities
(LEAs) 7–8, 10, 11, 137
Partnership Officers 65
programmes and initiatives 61–2

reduction of powers 130
local management of schools (LMS) 75, 157
Louis and Miles 100

Macbeath, J., Thomson, B., Arrowsmith, J. and Forbes, D. 54
mainstreaming good practice 65–7
Mansfield, M. 83
maths schemes, IMPACT project 107–9, 113, 114–15
Meighan, R. 143
MENCAP 133
Merttens, R. and Morgan, C. 113
Merttens, R. and Stockton, E. 39
Merttens, R. and Vass, J. 52, 106, 112, 114
Merttens, R. and Woods, P. 109
Metropolitan Life Survey 149
Minns, H. 19
Monson Primary School, New Cross, London 53
Mortimore, P., Hillman, J. and Sammons, P. 4
Mortimore, P. and Mortimore, J. 119
mothering,
models of 30–1, 32–3
and parental involvement 33–5
Mr Gumpy's Car 41
multimedia 19; *see also* video

National Children's Bureau,
survey of parent education 21
National Commission on Education 91, 106
National Consumer Council's Parents' Forum 2
National Curriculum 43, 58, 75, 157
National Home–School Development Group (NHSDG) 5
National Parenting Education and Support Forum 162
NCH Action for Children 15–16
Newham, London Borough of,
Action Guide for Schools 87–8, 93
home–school initiatives 89
parents' involvement and children's achievement 83–93
Parents in Partnership (PIP) 83, 85–93·
social profile 84–5
Newham Parents' Centre 84–5, 87, 92, 132
Nisbet, J. and Watt, J. 95
North Area College, Stockport 53
Not Now Bernard 41
nurseries and playgroups 23

O'Connor, Anne, and Harbinger Video Project 124–6
Office of Population Censuses and Surveys (OPCS) 152
OFSTED reports 5, 67, 68
parental consultation process 10
on poverty and under-achievement 91
on Section 11 work 63

oral traditions 40
Ostmo, Gavin, and Harbinger Video Project
120–4
outreach work 61
PACT home-learning scheme 17, 106
'Paired Reading' projects 51–2
Parent Link 21
Parent Partnership Scheme, Newham 83
Parent School Partnership (PSP), Liverpool,
    and confidence 74–5
    development 70–2
    evaluation 72–6
    five–year plan 76–8
    future plans 81–2
    organization 78–81
    Records of Achievement (ROAs) 75, 80
Parent Support Programme, Liverpool 70–1
Parent Teacher Associations 147
parent/client policy statements 13
Parental Involvement in the Core Curriculum
    (PICC) Project, Tower Hamlets 118
parents,
    accountability 8–9
    and achievement 1, 19–20
    agenda for 69
    arrangement for new parents 69
    changing expectations 1–2
    choice of school 11, 66
    communication with teachers 1–2, 19, 24,
        109, 112, 147–9
    as consumers 59, 130, 131
    and decision-making 129
    and decision-making by children 50, 51
    discouraged from involvement 10
    education levels 128
    entitlement to information 1, 59
    gender implications of involvement in
        schools 28–37
    on governing bodies 10, 66
    and homework projects 142
    increasing involvement in schools 28–9
    increasing pressures on 16
    involvement in secondary schools 139–50
    management role 12–13
    perceived as apathetic 139, 140–1, 143–5
    powers of 2
    pressure group activity 136–7
    role of 1
    role in parents' centres 132
    and school development plans 13, 43, 92
    support from schools for 17
    training for 15, 20–1, 30
    see also family
parents' centres,
    conflicting philosophies 132–3
    response to local needs 133–4
    role of parents 132
Parents' Charter 59, 130

parents' evenings 140, 146–7
parents' groups 21, 44–5, 58, 61
    Newham 84–5
Parents in Learning Society
    Project 60
Parents in Partnership (PIP), development 87
    Newham 83, 85–93
partnership ideals 3, 11, 23–4, 37, 60
Phillips, R. 85, 132
Phoenix, A. 31
Phoenix, A., Woollett, A. and Lloyd, E. 30
policy making, pupil involvement 49–50
poverty,
    in Newham 84
    in rural areas 154–6
    and under-achievement 91–2
Pugh, G. and De'Ath, E. 50–1
Pugh, G., De'Ath, E. and Smith, C. 21, 137
    Confident Parents, Confident Children 158,
        159, 160
pupil achievement agenda 64–5
pupils,
    attitudes to parents' involvement in school
        140, 145–7
    as clients 146
    involved in explaining curriculum 54
    involvement in school governance 49–51
    involvement with siblings' schools 51–2
    rights of 48–9
    target setting 53
    views of 54–5

questionnaires,
    Home School Employment Partnership
        (HSEP), Paisley 101–2
    of home–school work in Newham 88, 93
    Parent School Partnership (PSP), Liverpool
        73–6
    of pupils 54–5

racism 120
RAISE research project 104
REACHOUT (Routes into Education
    through Access in the Community and the
    Home) 80–1
reading with children,
    choice of books 41–2
    immigrant families and 39–45
    methods used 42
    role of siblings 51–2
    and sharing concept 41
    see also IMPACT project; literacy
Reading Recovery 91
reading schemes 42, 91
Records of Achievement (ROAs) 53, 75, 80, 146
resources,
    cuts in 58–9
    management of 5

utilising home learning 17–19
Robertson, P. 101
rural areas,
    definition 152–3
    economic and social changes 153–6
    home–school work in 157–62
    and information technology 160
    isolation of parents 156–7
Rural Development Commission (RDC) 153
Rush Common School, Abingdon 54

Sallis, J. 141
Sanderson, Stobart, Stoker, Whalley 45
Sandow, S. 130
school councils 49, 54, 147
school development plans 13, 43, 92
school inspections 1, 5, 58; see also OFSTED
Scott, G. 30–1
Scottish Office Education Department, New Life
    for Urban Scotland 96
secondary schools,
    home–school work in 4, 6, 52–4, 61–2,
        139–50
    inter–department communication 148–9
    parents' support of pupils 141–3
    perceptions of parent apathy 139, 140–1,
        143–5
    see also adolescents
Section 11,
    funding 59
    home–school liaison schemes 5, 62–3
self-criticism in development of home–school
    work 3, 60
self-study projects 24
'Shared Reading' projects 51–2
Sheath, G., and Harbinger Video Project 118–26
short-term home–school projects 95
siblings, as home–school mediators 51–2
Single Regeneration Budget 63, 90
Sir John Cass Foundation School, London 44, 45
Smith, T. and Noble, M. 91–2
special educational needs (SEN) 3
    assessment process 129
    Code of Practice 5, 47, 58, 64–5, 83, 130
    Guide for Parents 64
    parents' advice centre 132–7
    pressure group activity 136–7
    statements 65, 66
Stewart Headlam School, Bethnal Green 45
Stobart, T. et al. 158, 159
Stoker, D., Hegarty, M., Jordan, V., Jaffer, S.,
    Meredith, L., Whipps, M., Green, D. and Ooi,
    P. 43
story-telling 40, 44
support, in effective families 22

target setting 53
teacher-training courses 149

teachers,
    communication with parents 1–2, 19, 24, 87,
        109, 112, 140–1, 143–5, 147–9
    and empowerment of pupils 55
    influence on response to IMPACT work
        112–13
    perceptions of parent apathy 139, 140–1,
        143–5
    pupils as 111
    responsibilities for home–school work 61, 68
    training in work with parents 149
test scores, publication of 1
Times Educational Supplement 10
Tizard, Barbara and Hughes, Martin 20–1, 39,
    106
Tomlinson, S. and Hutchison, S. 128, 129
Topping, K. 52
Topping, K. and Wolfendale, S. 106
Tower Hamlets,
    Harbinger Video Project 118–26
    Parental Involvement in the Core Curriculum
        (PICC) Project 118, 119
    parents' advice centre 128–37
Tower Hamlets Deaf Children's Society 133
training,
    for governors 8
    INSET 5, 62, 65, 68, 77, 114
    for parents 15, 20–1, 30
    for work with parents 13, 149
transport, rural 152, 154
traveller education 3
Troyna, B. 56

UN Convention on the Rights of the Child
    (1989) 48, 50
Urban Programme 59, 60, 63, 77, 95, 96
Utting, D. 15, 16, 51

Veritas 21
video, making school more visible to parents
    118–26
village schools 157
Vincent, C. 132
violence against children 16
Vygotsky, L. 110–11

Walkerdine, V. and Lucey, H. 29, 30
Watkins, C. 146
Wells, Gordon 106
    The Meaning Makers 19–20
whole-class teaching 24
whole-school approach,
    to home–school work 66–7, 69
    to raising achievement 92
Wolfendale, S. 1, 3, 29, 58, 90, 93, 102
    All About Me 53
Wolfendale, S. and Topping, K. 92
work shadowing 101

Lightning Source UK Ltd.
Milton Keynes UK
13 March 2010

151311UK00001B/24/A